Get to the Sunshine

# Get to the Sunshine

Life Lessons that Brought Me
to the Western States Finish Line

Second Edition

Laura Chancellor

Get to the Sunshine - Second Edition



Cover and map design by Anna Martin Design
Cover photo by Kelly Valentine
Author photograph by Jill Andersen Photography
Book layout and production by Laura Chancellor
Editing by Alexis Nascimento

ISBN: 978-1-7343338-4-8
ISBN: 978-1-7343338-3-1 (ebook)

For Carol.

Of all the miles I've covered,
my favorite are the ones in these pages with you.
Thank you for everything you brought to this life.

Love, Your Prancing Unicorn

# CONTENTS

# WESTERN STATES ENDURANCE RUN
## Course Map & Elevation Profile

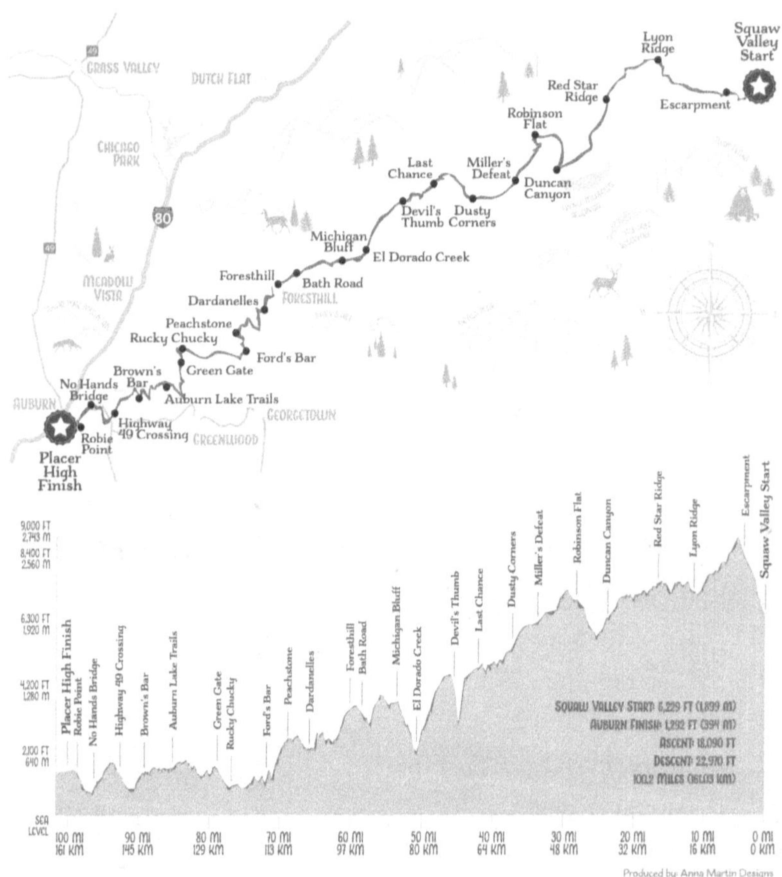

# FOREWORD
By Cathy Liu

My family moved to Durham when I was in the second grade. It was the second semester in January and I knew absolutely no one in my class. Durham is a blip on the radar and it was a very small town. Everybody already knew one another.

As I adjusted to life in Durham, I met Laura in elementary school. We lived one mile from each other and her father owned the dairy farm. I clearly remember when I went to Laura's house, we slid down the cottonseed pile on burlap bags. It was so much fun sliding among friends! In fifth grade, we both played the clarinet in Band, and in high school we marched along crowds of people in Disneyland Amusement Park twice. Laura and I also both participated in sports. Laura was a cheerleader while I played soccer. Both of us, however, ran Track and Field.

Laura and I had similar interests growing up. We loved overnight sleepovers, reading, shopping, and movie nights. I distinctly recall when we were in high school, we first watched "Titanic" starring Leonardo DiCaprio and Kate Winslet. Laura then re-watched it, I think, more than 10 times and she decided to replicate Kate Winslet's red gown with embroidered black lace for Junior Prom. She looked stunning!

After I graduated high school, I started to run again to ease the stress of my college workload and really loved it. I discovered it was my passion and my outlet to relieve tension and stress from my life. I really was intent on finishing my first marathon, so I summoned up my courage and started training for it.

The marathon came and it was exhausting and my whole body ached. My calves especially were in excruciating pain, but I finished in a little bit over four hours and I was proud of myself to have accomplished my goal.

After attending Emory University in Atlanta, Georgia for medical school, I decided to come back to Sacramento to start my residency at U.C. Davis, my alma mater. My first rotation was ambulatory care and I ran before going to work every day. After only two weeks into my residency, I was hit by a car during my morning run. Everything happened in a spilt second and my life was forever changed.
Within 24 hours, the neurosurgeons operated three surgeries on me at U.C. Davis Medical Hospital. After being in a coma and the swelling in my brain was reduced, I had to relearn everything all over again. I sustained traumatic brain injury and had to be taught how to speak and how to walk, but worst of all, I couldn't run. When Laura heard about my injury, she resolved to take up running because I couldn't.

I get very emotional every time I think of how Laura runs on behalf of me. Her determination and perseverance make me honored to call her my friend. All people see their lives in different ways depending on their own point of view. Either you see the glass half empty or half full or you are either a pessimist or an optimist. Laura and I agree on one thing - either you live your life fully with your friends and family loving you or die trying.

I know that every time she laces up her shoes and hits the pavement or trails, I am on her mind and for that I am eternally grateful. And while we may not run together at this moment in time, I am confident and determined to lace my running shoes up one more time!

# INTRODUCTION

The Western States 100-Mile Endurance Run came to life in 1974 when Tevis Cup participant Gordy Ainsleigh challenged himself to complete the course on foot alongside the Tevis Cup horses and their riders. The Tevis Cup "100 Miles – One Day" Ride, created by the Western States Trail Foundation, is a 24-hour equestrian event that still exists today. Horses and riders complete 100 miles of mountain trails from Squaw Valley to Auburn, California. Gordy Ainsleigh completed the 100-mile course in 23:42 that year.

The first official Western States Endurance Run was held in 1977 with 14 male participants. They ran alongside the horses and riders of The Tevis Cup Ride, with three of them finishing the event. The 30-hour finishers award was created this year after two of the finishers completed the race in more than 24 hours, but less than 30. In Fall 1977, the Western States Trail Foundation created the Western States Endurance Run Board of Directors. The following year, 63 participants started the race and the first female participant finished. In 1978 the race was moved to one month before the Tevis Cup and has since been held on the last weekend of June every year. One year later, the field grew to 143 runners and now reaches the full entrance field allotted each year.

Thousands of hopeful entrants qualify for the Western States Endurance Run year after year. To enter, runners are required to complete one of the qualifying races prior to entering the lottery. In 2015, the total number of entrants was 2,566 with the total number of tickets being 6,601. This year the $2^{(n-1)}$ formula was instated allowing entrants to obtain more tickets for each consecutive year they enter the lottery. (n = the number of consecutive years the entrant is in the lottery.) Previously, each entrant received one ticket for each consecutive year they were in the lottery.

In following years, the ticket counts have skyrocketed due to more consecutive years of being in the lottery and more entrants overall. As of writing of this book, the 2019 totals were 5,862 entrants and the total number of tickets at 20,119. The longest amount of time an entrant had been trying to obtain a spot in the race was seven years. Each year, there are 369 spots for the race. This includes sponsor spots, golden tickets, top 10 placements, aid station entrants, special consideration entrants and those lucky enough to be pulled from the lottery.

◆ ◆ ◆

Every year, the race starts at 5 a.m. on the last Saturday of June at Squaw Valley, California. Participants run 100.2 miles of mountainous terrain with 18,000 feet of elevation gain and 22,000 feet of elevation loss over the course of the race. They pass through 21 aid stations to complete the race before the 30-hour cutoff time.

There are strict cutoffs at several of the aid stations on the course. As the race progresses, race officials use cutoffs to make sure runners can make it to the finish line under the 30-hour time limit. These strict cutoffs allow the race directors to keep athletes who will be able to finish on the course, and pull those are too far behind pace to finish.

The finishing percentage fluctuates year over year based on many factors, the biggest being weather – ranging from extreme heat to residual snow on the course from the winter, and even hailstorms in the high country.

In 2015, the finishing percentage was 68.5% with 254 of 371 starters finishing. Temperatures that year rose to the 90s with the heat in the deep canyons being even higher. While Western States has always been an exciting race, it has gained momentum over the past few years with record-breaking race times and intense running conditions.

For more information on the Western States 100-Mile Endurance run, visit www.WSER.org.

# ONE
## Saturday, June 27, 2015 - 3:30 a.m.

*What is that noise?*, I thought when I heard my alarm go off at 3:30 a.m. The fluffy down comforter felt good snuggled up to my chin as the mountain air chilled my cheeks. I reached over with my foot and felt Joe next to me, still sound asleep. Then I remembered where I was.

"Oh my gosh, I'm running 100 miles today," I whispered.

I could feel the weight of that statement.

*This is the Big Dance*, I thought to myself. *Let's do this.*

I slowly and carefully crept out of bed as to not wake my boyfriend gently snoozing next to me. I quietly tiptoed across the room to the bathroom and turned on the light. Fluorescent light is never forgiving in the morning. The reflection looking back at me revealed tired eyes. The same tired eyes that had spent hours and hours training in the mountains over the past six months. The same tired eyes that had gone through tough times that nearly derailed my training and made today a day that wouldn't happen. The same eyes that wondered constantly if I would let everyone down today.

"I'm running Western States today," I whispered to my reflection. I pulled my long dark hair back into a loose ponytail, shut off the light and crept out toward the kitchen.

I heard my friend Andy, a member of my race crew, snoozing on the living room floor as I left the bedroom. My crew chief, Carol, was still asleep in the other bedroom. The Squaw Valley condo we had rented was small, but large enough for the four of us staying in it. In an attempt to not wake Andy, I carefully tiptoed across the room and flipped on the light over the stove. The soft, yellow glow gently illuminated the room allowing my eyes to adjust slowly. I opened the fridge, grabbing the strawberry jam and bread. I retrieved a butter knife from the silverware drawer, along with a paper plate and the peanut butter. As I started to make my favorite race day breakfast – a peanut butter and jelly sandwich – my mind began running through every possible thought that one could have before the sun comes up on race day.

*What time does the race start? Did I put everything in my pack that I need? Does my crew have all their instructions? What if I don't make it to the first aid station in time? Where are my shoes?*

I couldn't think straight. I spilled a bit of jam on the counter and reached for a paper towel to clean it up. That's when I felt it. The nagging pain in my low back. I knew I shouldn't have done anything new yesterday. Of course the one day I decided to take care of my body before a race by foam rolling, I hurt myself.

*Who does that?* I thought. *Who hurts themselves the day before the biggest race of their life?*

Thankfully in that moment, my coach Mo was at Squaw Valley with me and suggested rubbing Tiger Balm on the area to help relieve some of the pain. I could tell that I definitely needed to reapply this morning. I could only hope that this would help me stick it out through the next 30 or less hours.

I carefully wrapped my sandwich in a paper towel to eat later. The nerves were starting to kick in and eating was the last thing on my mind. Then I heard a voice.

"You're running Western States today."

It was Andy, still laying on the floor in the living room. We were old co-workers and knew each other from working in the advertising industry a few years back. He had started running after I bugged him about it enough, and while he was new to the ultra running scene, he was thrilled to be along for the crazy ride as a member of my crew.

"I am," I replied quietly with a small grin on my face. I saw his head pop up on the other side of the couch with a tired smile. "How did you sleep?" I asked.

"I slept OK. I'm more worried about you," he said. "How did you sleep?"

"Like a baby. Better than I thought I would," I answered. "Thank goodness the bed is super comfy here. I honestly don't know if Joe is going to wake up!"

Just then the bedroom door opened, revealing Joe's tall, slender frame in the doorway.

"Good morning," I said.

"You're running Western States today," he replied with a smile.

"I am," I affirmed as I walked over to kiss him. "It's going to be a great day."

Although Joe and I had only been dating for six months, it meant a lot for me to have him here with me on my big day. Joe was an Ironman triathlete and had run the 50K distance several times. Plus, he had crewed and paced at Western States in previous years, so he knew what we were up against for the next 30 hours.

I walked into the bedroom and turned on the overhead light. As was my tradition before every race, I had laid my race outfit on the floor last night before going to bed. I had all of the necessities: my sports bra, a neon yellow Fleet Feet Sacramento tank top, black shorts, red leg sleeves, grey socks, trail shoes, white cooling hat, white arm sleeves and my Garmin watch. I carefully got dressed making sure to apply Body Glide to any areas that might chafe. Then I opened the door to chat with my crew while I finished getting ready.

"Good morning, Western States runner!" Carol said as she popped into the bedroom.

"Morning!"

I was feeling nervous, but so glad to talk to Carol. At this point, being alone at all felt awful.

Carol was my crew chief. She had crewed me for a few other races and trained for ultra distance races with me. She knew exactly what I needed, how I operated and my personality when things got tougher in the late hours of a race. A race crew can really make or break your race experience. They have to be efficient, calm and good at trouble shooting. Runners rely on their crews to get them in and out of aid stations quickly, provide them with specific items discussed prior to the race and support them emotionally through the ups and downs of race day.

At Western States there are 10 potential crew stops along the course not including the start and finish lines. Because of the canyons, you can have a crew A and crew B for the race. One crew can go to stops on the near side of the canyon and the other would go to stops on the far side if you wanted to have crew at all the locations. I chose to have one crew go to the biggest stops along the course that day on the crew A route

"Did you put on sunscreen?" Carol asked me.

"Oh! I forgot. Will you put some on my shoulders?" Carol grabbed a bottle of sunscreen from our gear box, sprayed it on her hands and applied it to my shoulders, neck and ears.

I secured my cooling neck band around my neck as Carol snapped a photo of me. I don't know why I thought I needed to put on my cooling neck wrap that early. Must have been my nerves taking over. I pulled my ponytail through the hole in the back of my hat, tied my shoes and walked out to the living room.

"Joe?" I asked. "Can you to put some more Tiger Balm on my back?"

"Sure thing," he said. I brought the jar of ointment to him and he carefully rubbed it into the left side of my low back just above my running shorts.

"OK, let's make sure we have everything."

"We did that last night," Carol said.

"I know, I'm nervous and I need to do it again," I replied as I started checking my pack and bottles to make sure I had all my necessities for the first 30 miles. I knew I wouldn't have help from my crew until Robinson Flat – about 30 miles in – so I wanted to feel totally secure before leaving.

I counted six baggies of Skratch Labs Sport Hydration Drink Mix powder, three in each of my two handheld bottle straps, plus one serving mixed with water in each bottle. This year, I chose to consume my electrolytes through fluid instead of salt pills. I had trained with Skratch Labs Sport Hydration Drink Mix as electrolyte replacement for all my races since Javelina Jundred and it had worked really well for me.

*That should be enough for eight hours of running. I'll definitely make it to Robinson before then,* I thought.

I had stored a bunch of chews and energy gels in the pockets of my racing pack, along with some chips, crackers and trail mix. The back of my pack held a small baggie with first aid supplies (Band-Aids, blister tape and Tylenol), along with another stick of body glide.

I knew there would be three aid stations before I would see my crew so there were places to refill my Skratch and pick up additional snacks.

As I took a deep breath and looked around at the three faces staring back at me I thought, *I'm so lucky.*

"You ready guys?" I asked. They nodded in unison. "Let's do this."

I put on my pack while Andy grabbed my bottles and Joe picked up my sandwich off the counter. Carol grabbed my lightweight jacket, opened the heavy door leading to the hallway and gestured for me to lead the way through.

I took a deep breath and stepped out into the hallway headed for the start line of the Western States 100.

◆ ◆ ◆

As we walked out of the condo's automatic doors, I immediately felt the excitement in the air. There were runners and crew members everywhere you looked. Everyone was moving in the same direction, towards the base of the Squaw Valley ski lifts. Joe came up next to me, grabbed my hand and kissed it.

"You will do great today, babe," he said. "You got this."

"I know," I replied. "I'm super nervous."

I couldn't even smile I was so anxious and shaky.

"That's OK. Just keep moving forward," he reminded me. "Next step, grab your bib."

We walked along, past the entrance to the Base Camp gondola. Then past another condo building. Past the snow equipment rental area and snowboard repair shop. There were other runners and their crews walking alongside them. The previous excitement was slowly turning into a palpable, uneasy silence. As we got closer to the start line, the hum of the crowd became louder. I could feel excited, nervous energy bubbling from the start line around the corner, so I picked up the pace.

As we made the right-hand turn, I saw the tents with the bib pick-up lines. I walked up to the line for my 'L' last name and my crew stopped to wait for me. While I waited in line, I nervously checked the front pockets of my pack again.

*There are my energy gels. There are my chews. There are my emergency electrolyte capsules. Check. Check. Check.* I thought.

I peered down at my watch. Full battery. Good.

Then I felt it even more. Nerves. Nerves. Nerves. All I could feel were my nerves bubbling to the surface.

"Miss, what's your last name?" the volunteer asked.

"Oh, I'm sorry. Lots of nerves this morning," I responded. "It's Langerwerf. Laura Langerwerf. Bib number 1-2-6."

"May I see your wristband?" she asked.

"Sure thing," I said as I put out my right arm.

The volunteer checked my bib against my wristband confirming I was indeed runner number 126. I had chosen the number 1-2-6 for my birthdate, January 26. I had also run my qualifier, the Javelina Jundred, under the same bib number, so it just felt right.

"Here you go, Laura. Please do not fold the timing strip on the back of your bib. You must wear your bib at all times. Please attach the red timing chip to your shoe."

"Will do. Thank you," I replied.

"Have an excellent race!" the volunteer said with a bright smile.

I smiled back, took my bib, safety pins and timing chip and walked back to my crew.

"Get everything you need?" Carol asked.

"Sure did. Just have to put this all on," I said as my nerves continued to churn.

I carefully folded the sides of my bib in to make it skinnier to fit on my shorts. I used the four safety pins to attach it to my shorts while Joe illuminated my hands with his cell phone light. I stepped away to run a few strides up and down the sidewalk to ensure my bib was comfortable against my leg. Then I went about securing the timing chip to my shoe.

"I'm putting this on and attaching it with a safety pin," I told my crew. "When we change my shoes, we will need to remove this with the safety pin and put it on the new pair of shoes."

My crew chief Carol replied, "You got it sister. Chip on shoe always. Check." She smiled at me as she handed me my jacket.

*I can't believe I'm about to run Western States,* I thought.

"This is insane," I said out loud to my crew. I pulled the jacket on over my pack and glanced towards the start line. "Let's go over there," I said and began walking in that direction. My crew followed diligently, knowing that I was an anxious wreck.

We walked past the bib tents and through the packs of nervous runners and crew. The noise was incredibly loud at the start line. So many people talking, cheering, hugging, laughing. Everyone was amped! As I stopped nearby, Joe handed me my peanut butter and jelly sandwich.

"Time to eat, babe," he said, knowing that I'd need the energy.

I reluctantly took the sandwich and started nibbling at it. Eating was the last thing I wanted to do at this point, but I knew I had to get down at least half of the sandwich before the gun went off.

"Maybe I should wear this jacket for the first part?" I asked my crew.

"No, you don't need it," Carol said. "You will be warm as soon as you start climbing. Leave it with us."

"OK." I needed to hear that. My nerves were telling me all sorts of things I really didn't need to hear.

At five minutes to start time, my crew got ready to head up the Escarpment and take photos of me on the first section. This steep slope was the first climb along the 100-mile trek.

"You'll do great girl!" Andy said as he hugged me goodbye.

Carol took my jacket, gave me a squeeze and said, "We will see you in Robinson Flat! You got this!"

Joe kissed me goodbye. "I love you babe. Go get it! We will see you up the hill!"

He grabbed the last piece of my sandwich in the paper towel out of my hand to throw it away. I wasn't eating it anymore anyway.

With that my crew headed up the Escarpment to find a good spot to take photos of me. As I watched them disappear into the faint morning light with the hundreds of other spectators, suddenly I felt completely alone in a huge crowd.

I pulled my arm sleeves up and began taking deep, cleansing breaths.

*Don't be nervous.* I thought. *You know how to do this. You know what you are doing today.*

I looked around. There were about 350 other runners around me, chatting with each other, hugging and wishing each other well. Runners smiled nervous smiles and rocked side to side. Some stood still, arms crossed. Some smiled wide-eyed like they had drunk too much coffee. I smiled at those around me and tried to shake off the nerves myself.

*Today is just me,* I thought to myself. *I'm the only person who can run 100.2 miles. I have to believe in myself more than I've ever believed before.*

The challenge was to go the full distance. To take on the physical miles – the mental fatigue. To test all my limits over the course of 100.2 miles.

I gazed up at the sky that had started to lighten from the rising sun and thought, *I have to choose to believe. I have to choose to believe I can do this. I can do this. I know I can do this.*

I kept repeating those words to myself over and over. I thought back to the many, many times I had watched Western Time, a film by Billy Yang, and chose to believe in myself the way Sally McRae did when she ran her first Western States in 2014.

"This is all me," I whispered to myself as I turned my face up to the sky, closed my eyes and grinned. "I am running Western States."

As I lowered my face down and slowly opened my eyes, I saw the clock counting down from 30 seconds. The energy was electric. The nervous chatter started to subside. Everyone was glancing around wide-eyed. Smiles crossed the runners' faces around me as the clock ticked down. At 10 seconds to start everyone began loudly counting down with the clock.

"10, 9, 8, 7, 6…" and even louder yelling, "5, 4, 3, 2…1!!" The ceremonial shotgun blast went off and the elite runners tore through the start line arch with no hesitation. The 2015 Western States Endurance Run was under way and I was a part of it!

*Here we go!* I thought as everyone started moving forward.

We were a giant pack of runners being squeezed through a 20-foot wide starting chute. We took it at a slow jog for about 30 yards then the as trail narrowed, everyone began to walk onto the first ascent.

The air was crisp and clean. The sun was slowly illuminating the sky above us, which was now a light blue. The road we traveled up was lit with flood lights and lined with spectators for the first half mile. The route was a wide service road until we reached about a half mile from the Escarpment where it would turn into a single-track trail. There were coaches, crews, family members, friends, photographers and fans of the race all along the road. Cameras flashed as we made our way past everyone and up the mountain. I caught a glimpse of Joe and Andy on one side of the road as I hiked by. I gave them a wave and a smile knowing I would see them again soon.

*Conserve your energy,* I thought. *Don't let the excitement make you move too fast. Power hike to the top of the Escarpment. Stick to the plan.*

I knew there were no good places to run this part of the course. The first three or so miles were straight up to the top of the Escarpment near Watson's Monument. Only the elite and lead pack runners actually attempt running up most of the first few miles. A 2,000-foot gain in elevation was no joke.

*Just hike the way you have been practicing the past year and a half,* I told myself. I got in my good hiking stance, holding my handheld bottles at my waist and gently pumped my arms to help propel my legs in strong steps as I ascended the hill.

"Push through your heels. Engage your glutes," I said to myself as I gained momentum and started slowly cruising past other runners. "This is what you've trained for, to hike the uphills and run the downs and flats. You've got this. Now let's make some magic happen!"

After only a half of a mile, I was already feeling the effects of working out at altitude. I suffer from sports-induced asthma and knew this could become an issue, but didn't anticipate it affecting me so early.

*Just keep moving forward,* I thought. *Every step forward is one step closer to the finish and one step further from a cutoff. You've got this. Keep moving.*

About a mile in, the altitude really started to affect me and my pace began to slow.

*Keep breathing, Laura. Keep everything even. The top of the hill is coming, then you can enjoy the downhill on the other side.*

I kept my pace steady as I continued to move up the steep hill. The crowd I was hiking with was slowly dispersing out and I started to notice there were fewer and fewer people around me.

*Gosh, I must be slowing down a lot,* I thought. *Am I the last one out here?*

I glanced behind me and saw there were still several runners coming up the trail so I wasn't alone.

*This is so hard,* I thought. *This is way harder than I thought it would be.*

"Just breathe and believe," I said out loud to myself. "That's all you can do."

I knew I was close to the top of the Escarpment as I reached a few of the upper ski lifts. The top of the mountain is a great place to spectate the race if you have the energy to hike up before sunrise. I saw a couple other folks I knew hiking back down from the Escarpment and said hi as they passed.

I could hear some cheering and shouting up ahead, and quickly realized that I was almost to the top. The trail took a hard right-hand turn just past the last ski lift. The road turned into a rocky, single-track section that felt more like rock climbing than trail running. I traversed the rocky area and that's when I heard it. The voice of my friend Brad from Sacfit.

"Hey Laura!" Brad said. "Looking good!"

"Hey Brad!!"

I had never been so happy to see a familiar face. Brad ran me into the finish at Javelina Jundred in 2014, all while he was wearing a boot for an ankle injury. He took a photo of me as I came up the rocky section. I glanced up past him and finally saw the top of the mountain. There were tons of spectators at the top, cheering, yelling and taking photos.

*I'm almost there,* I thought. *Thank goodness!*

I hiked past Brad and gave him a weak smile.

"You're doing great! Keep it up!" he said with a bright smile back.

"Thanks Brad. I'll see you soon," I replied.

"Yes, you will!" Brad said.

After this climb, I couldn't deny that I was tired. I had my bottles resting on my hips and was just trying to keep putting one foot in front of the other. I had gone from 6,200 feet in elevation to 8,700 feet and was definitely feeling it.

"It's so hard to breathe up here," I said to myself. "What is going on? I didn't think it would be so hard to breathe."

That's when I started to doubt my preparation for this race. I had thought based on my training that I would be able to complete the race in 27-28 hours. After all, I had done my last 100 miler in 28 hours and I had trained much harder for this race. But I never considered the negative affects the altitude would have on my breathing.

*I'm going to do this,* I thought.

I was about 20 yards from the crowds now. They were yelling and cheering. There was a guy with a vuvuzela and several folks with cowbells. Some spectators were dressed up, some were jumping up and down and some were simply sitting waiting for their runners to come through.

I knew some of my Fleet Feet Sacramento co-workers would be at the top to greet me, including my final pacer, Bob. I looked around when I reached the top and saw one of my favorite co-workers. Ellisa, wearing a unicorn head with her arms spread wide, was ready to wrap me up in a well-deserved hug.

"Hey girl!" Ellisa shouted. "Welcome to the top!"

"Oh my gosh," I said exhausted as I fell into her hug. "I'm so happy to see you!"

"Good job!" she screamed. "You're running States!

"I know! This is crazy. And I'm so tired," I replied. "Where is the rest of the crew?"

"Bob, Annie and Diane are just around the corner on the other side of the hill," Ellisa replied.

I glanced at my watch. 1:18. My goal was to get to the top in 1:15 or less so I wasn't too far off. I also didn't have time to stay and chat.

"Great, thanks! I'll see you at the finish!" I said as I headed out along the trail.

I glanced back for a moment to take in the amazing sunrise view from the top of the mountain.

*Wow!* I thought. *This is unreal.*

I had crested the mountain and began running along the rocky, single-track trail. I could immediately breathe a bit easier since I was no longer moving uphill.

The view on the other side of the mountain was amazing. Mountain peaks peppered the horizon for miles and miles. The sunrise against the distant peaks was breathtaking, and the air seemed so still on the top of the mountain.

This part of the course was so high that there were fewer trees than I imagined. Most of the ground was covered by rocks and small, green shrubbery.

"Yay, Laura!" I heard someone yell. When I glanced up I saw Annie, Diane and Bob standing on the right-hand side of the trail waving.

"Hi guys!" I yelled back.

"You look great! You're right where you need to be," Diane said. She had run Western States a few years before.

"Way to go girl!" Annie yelled.

"I'll see you in a while, Bob," I said.

"You bet you will!" Bob replied. He would pick me up on the far side of the Rucky Chucky river crossing at mile 78 to pace me in for the last 22 miles of the race. Bob had run Western States before and was very familiar with all parts of the trail, and how to successfully run an ultra-marathon. I had asked Bob to pace me right after I qualified for the race given his expertise.

I grinned and waved as I passed by them on my way down the back side of the mountain.

# TWO

## Saturday, July 9, 2007

It was a warm summer evening in my hometown in northern California. I was there for the weekend visiting my family and some friends. Here I often found myself with Lindsay, my childhood best friend. We liked to gather at her house for vodka cranberry cocktails, nachos and great conversation.

"Do you want another vodka cran?" Lindsay asked me.

"Sure!" I replied. "Who doesn't want another vodka cran?"

Along with Lindsay, our friend Grant and I sat at her kitchen table catching up about life in Sacramento and back home. Lindsay and I had been friends since we were born and our older brothers were still best friends. We had been friends with Grant since preschool.

I watched Lindsay carefully pour cranberry juice over the ice and vodka when my phone rang.

"Hey, it's Kira!" I said excitedly. We all had known Kira since we were little and went to school together through high school.

"Hi Kira!" I exclaimed as I answered, already feeling our first round of drinks. "What's going on?"

Kira and I lived in Sacramento and chatted often. Coming from a small town, when you move to a bigger city you tend to gravitate towards those you know from home. It was comforting to know that she was so close by and we could get together on a moment's notice.

"Hi, Laura," Kira said in a somber voice. I could tell by her tone that something was wrong. "Cathy has been in an accident. She's in a coma in the hospital."

"What?" I responded, so confused.

Cathy Liu was one of our classmates, and she had sat next to Kira and me in the clarinet section in band. We also all took AP classes together. Cathy was a marathon runner, and it was common knowledge that she ran every single day. She was also in the second week of her medical residency at UC Davis Medical Center in Sacramento. Cathy had recently graduated from Emory University in Atlanta and came back home to start her medical career.

Cathy and I had met up for dinner about a week before at Zocalo in downtown Sacramento. We caught up on life, Cathy's boyfriend and her residency. We talked about our adventures in college and how our families were doing. I remember she had shown me her cute little Land Park apartment. It was so quaint and shone with Cathy's personality.

"What happened?" I asked.

Kira carefully replied, "She was out for a run and was hit by a car. I don't know anything else at this point, but I wanted you to know."

"Whhhhaat?" I said slowly, the shock rising in my voice.

"I know. I don't know what to do," Kira said choking back tears. "She had been missing for a few days and was a Jane Doe in the hospital."

"WHAT?!" I almost shouted back at her. "Are you serious?"

"Yes. I'm serious," Kira replied. I could tell she was crying now.

"I'm sorry. I know you're serious. I'm in shock. I just saw her last week," I said.

Tears began welling in my eyes as we continued to talk. My mouth hung open and I slowly began to relay the things Kira was saying to Lindsay and Grant. Their eyes got wider the more I talked.

Cathy was at the UC Davis Medical Center in the ICU. She had been hit by a car while out for her morning run in Land Park where she had her little apartment and was starting a life in Sacramento. Cathy was an avid runner and knew how to navigate the streets of a city. The driver didn't see her when the accident happened. Thankfully, the car had stopped and the paramedics were called right away.

Cathy didn't have any ID on her at the time of the accident. After her boyfriend hadn't heard from her for the whole day – they were supposed to meet for dinner – he went to her apartment and realized she wasn't there, but her phone, keys, wallet and work items were. The only thing missing besides her, were her running shoes. He called her parents and the Sacramento Police, who came to the apartment.

The police took down the information and said they would check the local jail and hospitals. When a second officer arrived in the early hours the next morning, he told her boyfriend that a car had hit a young Asian woman while she was jogging the previous morning. He asked if Cathy had a mole on her forehead and her boyfriend said yes. He immediately called her parents and they all made their way to UC Davis Medical Center to confirm it was her.

The rest of our night was a complete blur. How do you wrap your head around an accident like that? How do you fathom your friend lying in the ICU after being hit by a car? How do you even understand that this could happen to someone so close to you?

When I got off the phone with Kira earlier that night, she and I had decided to meet up and visit Cathy's father and mother in the hospital. We knew with Cathy being in the Neurosurgical ICU (NICU) we wouldn't be able to see her, but if we could see her family, we wanted to let them know we were close by and would help any way we could.

I spent the rest of the evening talking with Lindsay and Grant. We wondered what we could do, how we could help… anything. But all we could do was wait to find out next steps.

On July 11, Kira, our friend Alyssa and I met at UC Davis Medical Center and made our way to the Neurosurgical ICU.

"Have you talked to Cathy's parents?" I asked Kira as we walked into the hospital.

"I have," she responded. "They are up on the ICU floor in a waiting room with Cathy's sister. They said to come by there when we get here."

We took the elevator up to the ICU floor and made our way past the locked doors of the unit. Kira knocked on the waiting room door and Cathy's mom came over to open it.

"Hello!" she said in her usual excited voice, as she hugged each of us. "Thank you for coming." We made our way into the room, giving

Cathy's dad a hug as well. Cathy's sister was sitting on a couch on the other end of the room and got up to welcome us.

They had some care packages other friends had brought to them with magazines, snacks and other small comforts. The residents in Cathy's group had also provided meals to make sure her family were taken care of. Cathy's family appeared tired but seemed optimistic, as they always were when we were growing up. They let us know they were staying at Cathy's apartment in Land Park while she was in the hospital.

Her parents explained to us that Cathy was in critical but stable condition in the Neurosurgical ICU. The doctors had her in a heavily sedated coma in order to help her heal. She still needed to be connected to breathing tubes and was receiving substantial pain medication. The doctors were also taking early precautions for her rehabilitation process by putting special boots on her to prepare her legs for walking in the future.

"We are so glad you girls live so close to her and are here to support her," her mom said. "It means so much for you to have come by to see us."

"We wouldn't have it any other way," I responded. "If there is anything we can do to help or anything we can bring to you, please let us know."

"Oh, we will," her dad responded. "You know we will."

"We will come by 2 or 3 days a week if that's ok with you guys?" I said. "We can come get updates and pass them on to the folks back home. I will also bring any cards or emails folks have sent to us for you and Cathy."

"That sounds great," her dad responded. "We will be here."

Kira, Alyssa and I made our way out of the hospital, walking mostly in silence. Hearing Cathy's status hit us a lot harder than we had anticipated. We exited through the emergency room and into the sunshine.

"Well, that was interesting," I said.

"It was kind of surreal," Kira responded.

"I'm glad to hear she's doing as good as can be expected!" Alyssa said, always optimistic.

"I'm so glad we all went together. Thanks for coming," I said to my friends. "This is just…" and I couldn't get anything else out.

Alyssa continued to chat as we walked to our cars, but I don't remember what we talked about. Knowing our friend was laying in the hospital had me so confused and honestly, frustrated.

"Alyssa, I know you have to go back home, but Kira, when do you want to come back this week?" I asked.

"Let me check my calendar and get back to you! Definitely this week," she said.

The next time we visited Cathy's family in the hospital, I met Kira a few blocks away where we parked our cars. Each time we visited we would catch up on our days and share any news we had received from other friends who had stopped by the hospital. We would make our way up to the Neuro ICU and meet up with Cathy's parents and sister. They were always so welcoming and happy to share Cathy's status.

Over the next month we visited the hospital a few days a week. Then Kira and I found out we would be able to see Cathy in person as she had been moved to her own room out of the ICU. We were elated!

"Do you believe we get to see her?" I asked Kira as we were walking up to the hospital.

"No. And I'm kinda nervous," she responded. "I wonder what she will look like."

"I'm sure she will look like the same old Cathy," I said with a smile. On the inside I was so nervous, but in these situations I tended to support those around me so my nerves wouldn't come through.

When we arrived at her room Cathy's mom welcomed us in. We came around the curtain and Cathy was propped up slightly in bed with her boyfriend standing next to her. Cathy's hair had been shaved due to her many brain surgeries. The front left side of her head was a bit indented in, as they had temporarily removed a section of her skull to allow for brain swelling, and her three brain surgeries in the first 24 hours she was in the hospital.

The minute Cathy saw us her eyes lit up the way they always had before. I remember immediately thinking *She knows who we are! Yes!* I carefully followed Kira to the foot of her bed.

"Hi Cathy!" Kira said in a sweet, but excited voice.

"You look great!" I said to Cathy. "We are thrilled to see you."

"We've been coming to the hospital throughout the weeks to see your family and get updates," Kira stated. "They've been keeping us up to date on your progress."

I nodded alongside Kira. At this point Cathy couldn't speak at all. She was making great strides in her recovery though. Cathy was responding to cues such as holding up fingers, moving her fingers in a counting motion when asked and squeezing someone's hand in response to a question. She was also holding and looking at the get well cards people had sent to her. At this time she was off the breathing machine, though she was still not eating on her own as she couldn't swallow.

We talked with Cathy's mom and boyfriend for a few minutes before we headed out.

"It was so great to see you, Cathy," Kira said.

"I know I said it, but you look great," I added.

I led Kira into the hallway to chat with Cathy's mom and get an update on her progress at this point. When we stepped out the door, I turned around to face Kira as she burst into tears. We stood there in the hallway hugging each other for a bit, not really understanding where our reactions were coming from, but understanding at the same time. Seeing our friend in such a vulnerable situation was so difficult. And the worst part was that we couldn't fix it no matter how hard we wished we could.

Our walk back to the car was quieter than usual.

"What are you thinking?" Kira asked me.

"She's doing good!" I said, trying to keep it positive. It was so hard to see our friend going through this. "I am so glad her family is here to be by her side through all of this."

"Me too," Kira replied quietly. "I'm glad we're here for her too."

We continued to visit her family in the hospital a few times a week and provide updates to folks back home. In most cases, we weren't able to see her in person due to tests being performed or that she was taking a nap. Finally on August 21, a few weeks after our first in-person visit, we got to see Cathy again.

Kira and I were greeted with the biggest smile from Cathy when we entered the room. She smiled and mouthed the word "Hi" to us as we came around the curtain.

"Hi Cathy!" we both said, waving to her. She was propped up in bed again and looked even better than the last time we saw her. We could tell she had progressed so much in a short period of time.

We said hi to Cathy's boyfriend and took a seat in two chairs at the end of her bed. The room seemed brighter on this visit than the last time we saw her. Maybe it was Cathy's smile, maybe it was the sun outside, but the room was shining. We stayed at the hospital over an hour talking to her and her boyfriend, literally discussing everything we could with our friend. She did her best to gesture to us when she understood what we were saying. We were even more excited to see she was back eating real food and she even ate all of her dinner while we were there.

On Saturday, September 8 we visited the hospital for Cathy's 26th birthday party. Her family had reserved a meeting room where they had decorated and provided a cake and snacks for all of us. It was so great to see her with her fellow residents too. Alyssa was able to make the trip down to join us as well. Seeing Cathy living a more normal life, even though she was still in the hospital, made me so happy.

On Tuesday, September 25, almost three months after her accident, Cathy was released from the hospital and walked out by herself with her parents by her side. She was still doing therapy several hours a day including physical, speech and occupational and had a long road to recovery.

Cathy is now back living a normal life on her own. These days she speaks to other traumatic brain injury survivors and shows so much optimism for the future. She is still her spunky, fun self and is looking forward to greater opportunities in the time ahead.

◆ ◆ ◆

Cathy was running when she was hit by a car. She was a gifted runner. She had been on our track team in high school and continued to run for recreation in college. Cathy had completed one marathon at the time of her accident. When I realized that it would be a long time until Cathy got a chance to run again, I decided that I needed to start running for her. That same year, I had been dating a guy whose sister-in-law was a runner. Megan had run the California International Marathon (CIM) in Sacramento. She told me that she trained with a group called Sacfit and they practiced the Galloway Method. This is a run-walk interval method where you run for a certain amount of time then walk for a certain amount of time, over and over again throughout your race. When she explained it to me, I realized that I may actually be able to run a marathon for Cathy if I tried. On July 15, 2007, I woke up and realized that it was time to make that goal happen.

*Where are my running shoes?* I thought to myself as I looked in my closet.

Back then, I usually bought my shoes at a big box store and always had to find them in the men's section because my feet were so big. (I wear a women's size 11 running shoe.)

"Here they are," I said to myself as I pulled them from the back of my closet. They were gray and black with a little bit of red, and not very pretty. I always hated that I could never run in cute shoes because I had to wear guys' shoes.

*This is going to be interesting,* I thought as I laced them up. *You got this, Laura. This is for Cathy.*

That day I laced up my shoes and started running for the first time in my life. I took it very easy in the beginning. I ran a two-minute run and one-minute walk interval to start out since I had no idea how long I'd actually be able to continually run.

My goal was to run a couple of miles around the lake in my neighborhood.

"You got this," I said to myself as I struggled to catch my breath in the first mile. I had mapped a 2-mile distance online so I would know how far to run that day. At the halfway point when I turned around, I was struggling.

*You've got this Laura,* I reminded myself. *Do it because Cathy can't.*

I finished my first run and knew I had my work cut out for me. I continued running a few days a week and within a the first few weeks I noticed pain in my knees when I was running. My brother, a physical therapist, told me it could either be a patellar tendon issue or I could need new shoes. I had never thought that shoes could be the issue, so I looked into getting some new ones.

I had heard about Fleet Feet Sacramento before then (we had a Fleet Feet back home in the nearby town of Chico) and decided I'd go down to the local store and get fitted for proper shoes.

I walked into the store that day, and felt a little out of place at first. As I wandered towards the shoe area, a nice guy smiled and walked towards me.

"My name is Justin," he said extending his hand. "How can I help you today?"

Immediately feeling more at home, I responded, "I need some running shoes."

"Well, you've come to the right place," he said. "Come with me."

We walked to the shoe floor where he sat on a fitting stool and I sat on a long bench.

"Go ahead and take off your socks and shoes for me," he said. "What kind of running are you doing?" he asked as he pulled out a measuring device I had seen in department stores.

"Well, I'm starting small. Just around 2 miles right now. Nothing big."

"What's your ultimate goal?" he asked.

"Well, I want to run a marathon eventually," I replied, and began explaining Cathy's accident and my purpose for running to him.

"That is a great reason to run a marathon," he said. "I know your friend will be proud."

"Thank you!" I replied, glad he thought it was a good idea, because I was still concerned about the whole thing.

"Go ahead and stand up on here for me," he said. I stood on the measuring device and Justin told me that my feet measured a women's 10 and 10.5 regular width. "Go ahead and come with me so I can watch you walk," he said. We walked to an open area of the store and Justin watched me walk about 20 feet and had me walk back. We went back to the bench and he told me that I had a neutral foot, which meant nothing to me at the time.

"I'm going to go grab some shoes for you to try on, OK?" he asked.

"Sounds good!" I replied. The store was bustling with action at that time. There were runners everywhere.

*This is really cool,* I thought to myself.

When Justin came back he had three different boxes of shoes for me to try.

"I found three pairs of shoes that I think you will like. Let's try the first one," he said.

When he opened the first box, I quickly sucked in my breath.

"Are those pink shoes?" I asked.

He chuckled and said, "Yes they are."

In awe I replied, "I've always worn guys' shoes. I've never gotten to wear girlie shoes before."

Justin smiled and said, "well, let's take these for a spin. Go ahead and run down to the door and back."

I stood up and took that first pair of shoes through the store. They were perfect. They felt great under my feet, and my knees didn't hurt at all. I'm not sure if that was due to the shoes or the simple fact that I was elated to wear girlie shoes, but I was on Cloud 9 in them.

After that day I never bought running shoes from another store. I knew what fit me. I knew the staff at Fleet Feet Sacramento knew what they were talking about. I continued to shop there for my running shoes for years and eventually worked for the company.

Four months later in October, I ran my first official race in Sacramento. I did the 5K distance (3.1 miles) at the Cowtown Marathon, now known as Urban Cow. This would set the stage as I started training for my full marathon. My plan was to train the rest of 2007 and slowly increase my mileage. Then I would volunteer at the 2007 CIM and after that train to run the CIM in December 2008.

I told Cathy I had started running because of her and she seemed flattered. I continue to run miles of each of my races for her. I don't think I'll ever stop doing that actually. Cathy told me one time that she would run a 5K with me someday. I am still praying and holding out hope that we will be able to accomplish that goal together one day.

◆ ◆ ◆

While Cathy couldn't join me at the Western States race, I believe she was sending me good thoughts while I ran the hardest 100 miles of my life. She knows what facing obstacles feels like. I can't imagine going through the things she's gone through and coming out on the other side as healed as she is. It's truly a miracle.

Cathy's situation taught me to stay optimistic about life. And to never take life for granted. You never know when it may change in the blink of an eye. If and when things happen to you or change in your life, it's important to make the best of the cards you've been dealt. Whether that's an injury, a breakup, losing someone you love… you have to make the best of that situation. And when you do that, you will be able to keep moving forward. When a wrench is thrown in your life, you can't throw in the towel. You have to stand up and keep the wheels turning.

# THREE

## Saturday, June 27, 2015 – Mile 3 - 6:50 a.m.

As I ran down the hill past Bob, Diane and Annie, I was finally able to catch my breath a bit and take in the view around me. It was breathtakingly gorgeous on top of the mountain. The sun had just come up over Lake Tahoe and was illuminating the mountains ahead of us. I felt like I was on top of the world. At that altitude the trees were scarce, so I could see all the way down into the canyon on my left. The well-worn trail stretched out in front of me, twisting and turning its way towards Auburn.

I had never been to this part of the course. The farthest I had ever been was up to Robinson Flat where the mile 30 aid station was located. I had never seen miles one through 30. The ground was much rockier than I imagined it would be and the trail had an almost chalk-like consistency. The shrubs on either side were small, one to three feet tall, and yellow and white wildflowers appeared among the greenery on the mountain.

As I cruised along the trail, I started to notice that my breathing wasn't getting any easier. I had hoped that since I wasn't climbing uphill, I would be able to catch my breath, but I wasn't that lucky. The altitude at the top of the hill had already taken a toll on my lungs and my labored breathing was starting to cause a bit of burning in my throat that I was hoping would go away. I also started to drink my fluids more than I had planned.

*Man, the altitude is a lot harder than I anticipated. When do I get to come down from this mountain? Shouldn't we be getting lower in altitude by now? What is happening to my breathing?*

These were all questions that kept running through my head as I made my descent down the mountain. What I didn't realize was that it wasn't really a descent. I was only dropping a couple hundred feet, not nearly what I needed to be back to breathing normally. Along with that I was running low on fluids.

This year was the first year the race directors and board had done away with the aid station at the top of the Escarpment at mile three. From the start line, the mileage to the first aid station was now 10 miles.

When I planned out my hydration, I figured that two 20-ounce bottles of fluid would be plenty to get me to the first aid station at 10 miles. I don't know why I thought that, considering I was planning to run a 15-minute average for that portion of the race. I typically consume 20 ounces of water or electrolyte every hour in my training and racing. But by the time I had gotten 4 miles into the race, my first bottle of fluid was already depleted. I had 6 more miles at altitude to ration one bottle of electrolytes.

When you exercise at altitude, the air is thinner, your body works harder and your breathing rate goes up, therefore you need to consume more fluid and more calories. I hadn't considered this when I planned my fueling and hydration. I hadn't done any altitude training, thinking I'd be just fine. I also hadn't planned on the hike up the Escarpment taking so long so I found myself in a bit of a panic trying to conserve the small amount of electrolyte drink I had left.

"Just keep moving and breathing," I kept telling myself. "You've got this, you just need to make it to Lyon's Ridge." I pulled an energy gel out of my pack, ripped off the top and began to eat it. I knew I had to keep myself fueled as much as possible, especially with how taxed my body was at this point.

The course continued along the side of the mountain with some easy rolling hills. The ground became rockier along the course, and I noticed a lot more water flowing down the trail than I had thought there would be, leaving my feet pretty wet. The weather that year had left us with not a lot of snow melt, so things were pretty hot and dry come race day, minus that water flow.

*I really hope this water doesn't affect my feet,* I thought. I was not prone to blisters at all. My feet were well calloused as a runner and I was able to run with wet or hot feet and be just fine. But this early into the race, I didn't know if the wetness would actually end up being my demise.

There were a few wooded areas we passed through with lots of tree coverage and bushes, but I noticed that most of the terrain was barren or covered with smaller bushes and shrubs at the altitude. I had imagined more forest like trees, but of course I hadn't taken into account the altitude before either.

"Just keep moving forward and breathing," I kept saying to myself. "You got this. You can do this. Remember, every step forward is one step closer to the finish and one step further from a cutoff."

I had been cruising along at a good clip and passed a few runners. While breathing was still a struggle, I was feeling a bit better as I was getting more used to the altitude. That's when I caught up with the original Western States finisher, Gordy Ainsleigh. He was the first to run the race back in 1974 and continues to run it each year that he qualifies. He's a legend in the sport and while he does have to qualify every year, he gets an automatic spot in the race if he does. We ran along together for a little bit and talked about what a nice day it was. We shared some good conversation and he wished me luck as I slowly pulled away from him.

The trail had turned into a wider fire road we followed across the top of the mountain. I looked at my watch and saw that I wasn't far from the aid station. I stopped on the side of the trail to relieve myself behind some bushes as a few runners passed by.

*Good, I'm hydrated. I'll make it to the aid station and be able to fill my bottles,* I thought to myself. *Just keep moving, keep pushing. You got this.*

One good sign in an ultramarathon is being able to go to the bathroom. That means you are hydrated and your body systems are all in working order.

I hopped back on the trail and made my way to the Lyon's Ridge aid station at mile 10.3. The aid station is at the top of a mountain in an open area where the fire roads come through. It's the only accessible place for the aid station, and volunteers must use 4-wheel drive or all-terrain vehicles to get in. As I approached the aid station I started to walk and removed the tops from my bottles to have them filled with water and my Skratch powder.

"Welcome to Lyon's Ridge! What can we help you with?" the aid station volunteers yelled cheerfully as I came in.

"Can you fill these with water for me?" I said as I handed them my two handheld bottles.

"Sure thing! Do you want a snack?" they asked.

"I'll take some of these chews," I responded, grabbing a sleeve of Clif Bloks and tucking them in the pocket of my hydration pack. "Do you have Coke?"

"You got it!" the volunteer replied as she handed me some Coke in a paper cup.

"Thank you," I said, exhausted.

I grabbed a Clif Shot energy gel in Vanilla flavor and tore open the package, eating it quickly. It tasted like vanilla frosting, quite possibly the best vanilla frosting I had ever eaten, but then I figured I was just hungry. I had been fueling plenty over the past few hours, but my plan was to try to eat 150-200 calories extra at every aid station, regardless of whether it was time to fuel or not. When I train and race, I consume 100-150 calories every 40 minutes. This has always been the key to keeping my energy up and my brain functioning well. I knew that I may miss a fueling or get off my calories during the race so if I kept eating when food was available it would help me keep going. I threw away the energy gel wrapper in the trash, and tucked an extra one in the front pocket of my pack.

One thing they tell you not to do on race day is to try anything new. However, when I run ultras, I always go with my gut. If something offered at an aid station sounds good, I eat it. If my body wants chips, I take some. If it wants cookies, I'm all about it. I figure that whatever my body is craving is what my body needs at that point. This day I tried the Vanilla Clif Shot gels for the first time and they are still my favorite years later.

I sipped the Coke and felt like I was in heaven. It tasted so good that I drank the whole cup and asked the volunteer for a refill which she gladly gave me. I grabbed some Fritos Big Scoops chips and started chomping on them. They tasted like the best salty snack on the planet! I could feel the grease on my fingers and the salt sticking to my lips as I started devouring on them. I noticed that they were breaking down easily and not drying out my mouth the way potato chips had in the past. *This is a great trail snack*, I thought as I put the last few in my mouth.

"Here you go!" the volunteer said as she handed my bottles back.

"Can you give me a hand putting this powder in these?" I asked her.

"Sure! When you get to the next aid station just tell them exactly what you need and they will fill them with the powder for you too."

"Thanks! That's good to know," I replied.

I had pre-packed baggies of Skratch in Matcha Green Tea & Lemon and Raspberry flavors for the day. I had trained with these flavors and the Matcha Green Tea & Lemon had some caffeine to keep me going the whole time. Three small baggies of Skratch powder were tucked into each of my handheld zipper pouches. That provided me with six refills of Skratch for six additional hours of moving, plus the two full bottles I started with. This was the plan for each time I saw my crew – Joe was in charge of adding the baggies to the zipper pouches so I always had plenty to make more bottles of electrolytes. I wouldn't run out of electrolyte mix that way and if I missed my crew somewhere, I would still have what I needed until I did see them.

"Do you need anything else?" she asked.

"I think I'm good," I said.

"Great! You're about five miles from Red Star Ridge. Have a great race!" she said cheering me out of the aid station.

"Thank you!" I yelled back as I made the left-hand turn out onto the fire road.

I checked my watch. I was 2:56 into the race, which was 7:56 a.m. The 30-hour time for Lyon's Ridge was 7:40 a.m.

*Shit!* I thought. *I'm already 16 minutes behind the 30-hour time. How did that happen? This isn't part of my plan. Dang it.*

I kept running and doing math in my head trying to figure out what happened. But nothing had happened. I had simply been running the race I should have been, I was just a lot slower than I had estimated. The altitude was really taking its toll and it was very evident based on the times.

I started to get worried about how I was going to make up time. I kept asking myself how this happened. Then I finally realized that dwelling on it wasn't going to help anything. All it was doing was stressing me out when I needed to focus on getting to the next aid station under the 10 a.m. cutoff. If I didn't make it by that cutoff, my race would be over.

In Western States, there are strict cutoffs at many of the aid stations. This is because as the race progresses, they can't have runners out on the course who can't realistically make it to the finish line under the 30-hour time limit. At a certain point you can't make up any deficits based on the terrain and mileage, so cutoffs allow the race directors to keep a handle on how many athletes will be able to finish versus the ones who will need to be pulled because they are just too far behind.

The trail, while still rocky, had become sandier as I continued along. The trees were getting larger and there were bushes and shrubs scattered about. Coming across the top of Lyon's Ridge, there were some spectacular views across the mountains. The trail runs along the ridge for a bit, and you can see for miles and miles on both sides. I felt like I was on top of the world looking out across the vast openness. I tried my best to take it all in as I knew something like this was so special to see. I took a moment to walk and open a pack of Clif Shot Bloks while I took in the view. I will never forget what physically being on top of the world felt like at that point. I ate several of the bloks as I walked and tucked the rest in my pocket.

I cruised along and after about a mile I saw some photographers up ahead on a rock formation. I didn't know at that time that I was approaching Cougar Rock, the famous rock the Mountain Lion is standing atop on the Western States finisher's buckles. The trail was pretty smooth leading up to Cougar Rock. As most runners do, I was prepared to smile at the photographers but when I got to the bottom of Cougar Rock I realized it would be an interesting climb to the top.

At the base of Cougar Rock the ground started to get really uneven with the rocks almost cemented together making a giant, steep formation. I grinned the best I could as I climbed up the rocks using my hands for stability on my way to the top. When I finally got there, I managed a weak smile for a photo, said hello to the photographers and went on my way. I was now a few miles from the Red Star Ridge aid station.

"I just have to keep moving and I will get there," I told myself. I'd check my watch over and over to make sure I was moving at a good pace, but I really couldn't go any faster because my breathing was still so labored from the altitude. I made sure to keep my feet moving at a good cadence even if my steps were short.

Just before Red Star there are a few long switchbacks down the mountain. I took those quick but easy, not charging them too hard. I needed to avoid blowing out my quads this early in the race. Many runners take the steep downhills at the beginning of the race really hard and fast, over using their quads, which causes them to not be able to run downhills by the end of the race. I was trying my hardest to avoid that.

*Like a gazelle, Laura. Dance down the hill,* I thought as I allowed my feet to pitter-patter through the dirt. I could hear the aid station at the bottom of the hill. There was a lot of chatter, music and noise as volunteers got everyone ready with their drop bags and items. I came in and went straight for the food table.

"How can I help you?" a volunteer asked. "Do you have a drop bag?"

I had only gone through one of my handheld bottles with Skratch so I handed it to her and asked, "Can you fill this bottle with water and one of the pouches of powder in the zipper pocket? And no, I don't have a drop bag, but thanks."

"Sure thing!" she responded and disappeared.

*Wow, it worked. The volunteers will help us with anything!* I thought.

I stepped over to the food area and grabbed some Fritos and Oreo cookies. I also had a handful of M&Ms and grabbed a few more Clif Shot gels and Clif Bloks for my pack. As I snacked on the M&Ms and chips, the volunteer came over with my bottle filled with ice cold Skratch. I smiled a weak smile at her as she put her hand on my back.

"Do you need anything else?" she asked with a bit of concern in her voice.

"No, I'm OK, just tired," I replied.

She gave me a smile showing that she understood. "You've got this," she said. "It's about 8 miles to Duncan Canyon. You sure you have everything?"

"Yeah, I'm good," I replied as she gently directed me out of the aid station.

As I started walking with three Oreo cookies in my hand, I yelled back, "Thank you all for being here!" and a few volunteers yelled back, "You're welcome!"

On my way past the final row of trash cans I walked by the radio tent where they were calling in runner numbers and times for online tracking and the race officials. I looked at my watch. It read 4:37. It was 9:37 a.m. The cut-off for this aid station was 10 a.m., but the 30-hour time to reach this aid station was 9:10 a.m. I was behind by 27 minutes now. I had lost 11 more minutes in just three miles.

I started a slow trot as I got further away from the aid station. *I feel like I keep getting kicked when I'm already down,* I thought. *Why can't I gain some time? Why am I not going faster? Why am I not good at this?*

That's when the first moment of true uncertainty popped into my head, as much as I hated to think it. *I don't know if I'm going to be able to finish this race.*

# FOUR
## Sunday, October 14, 2012

I remember the day vividly. It was a day that truly changed my life forever.

Despite the chill of the morning, the weather forecast was slated to be nice and sunny as the day went on. I was running a half marathon that day with my friend Kelly.

I woke up with a pit in my stomach. I had barely talked to my fiancé over the past few days. He was very distant and I felt like something was off. He would be running the race that day, but he didn't want to go to the race together. As I had done over the past four years of our relationship, I just went with it and took it as if it were normal even though I felt like we should go together. I mean, shouldn't my fiancé actually like to hang out with me before a big race?

That morning I drove down to the race early to get a good parking spot. As I walked towards the start line, I couldn't help but wonder what the heck was going to happen today. Things were off.

WAY off. And I could feel something terrible looming. But I put on the happy face and kept moving forward.

"You got this. You've got a race to run. Let's go," I told myself as I walked over to meet up with Kelly in the start area.

"Hey Kel," I said as she gave me a hug.

"Hey! How are you doing?" she asked gingerly. I know she could tell something was wrong.

"Something is wrong. I don't know what happened but something is wrong," I cried. "I have barely talked to him and I just have this awful feeling."

"I'm sure everything is OK. When is the last time you talked to him?" she asked.

"Yesterday we texted and he said he didn't want to come down here with me. He said he would come by himself," I responded. "Something is going to happen. I know it."

I told myself that I wouldn't look for my fiancé while I was waiting to start the race. That I would just give him the space he needed and hope things would be OK. But I couldn't help myself... I looked everywhere for him. As I tried to glance around nonchalantly, I anxiously twirled my one-carat princess cut diamond engagement ring around my finger. The pit in my stomach got heavier and heavier.

◆ ◆ ◆

Things had been off for a while. We had been arguing more than we should have been, and were on each others nerves all the time. Deep down I knew something was wrong because I couldn't even bring myself to order our wedding invitations. I had already said yes to a dress and paid deposits on a venue, photographer, caterer and florist – but something stopped me from planning our wedding any further.

We had been dating for more than four years after a chance meeting. We connected immediately after finding that we had similar upbringings being from small towns and growing up on ranches. We went on our first date a few weeks after we met and it seemed like a match made in heaven.

We started spending all our time together. I finally felt like I had found the person who aligned with my life. We were country, athletic, loved music, our parents were still married, we shared the same faith - the list went on and on. It was supposed to happen. Maybe that's why I fought so hard for it to continue for so long.

We broke up a few times throughout our relationship. It was tumultuous at times. While it was hard, we kept coming back together and I told myself this was how hard relationships had to be in order to be good. Surprisingly, it was during one of our "breaks" that he told me he really wanted a future with me. That I was his forever. We shopped for an engagement ring a few months later, and a few months after that, he proposed. I knew this was how the "fairytale" was going to continue forever and I was elated.

◆ ◆ ◆

Back at the half marathon, Kelly gave me a hug and said, "I'm sure things will be OK. Just breathe. We have a race to run. Let's focus on that!" She was always so upbeat and positive. Kelly had been a great friend through all the craziness of the relationship and was going to be a bridesmaid in our wedding. She was also the only friend who, when things got tough with him, honestly asked me if he was the man I wanted to marry. She's that friend. The one who will risk an entire friendship to ask the really hard questions, knowing that even if the friendship fails, she did the right thing. She's the kind of friend you want in your corner when things go south.

Kelly put a smile on my face and drug me to the starting corral. I checked my pack to make sure I had everything. We listened to the Star Spangled Banner, the gun went off and we headed down the course.

I wasn't expecting much from the day. I knew I wanted to maintain a good pace, but with everything weighing on my heart I just hoped to keep putting one foot in front of the other. We moved along through the streets of town. About halfway through the race, Kelly and I realized that if we turned our pace up a notch we would run a half marathon PR – personal record time – at the race. So we sped up the pace and started pushing each other. I was so grateful for this new focus during the race. It made pit in my stomach more tolerable.

We came into the finish just a few minutes off of our half marathon PR time! We were so close and immediately started talking about how we should have gone faster earlier, then we would have gotten the PR. We took some photos together and got ready to leave the race location.

That's when I saw my fiancé, waiting on the other side of the post-race food. I could tell he wasn't happy. I excitedly waved at him and made my way around the tables to the lawn.

As I quickly walked up to him, he didn't start to smile like I expected. He looked like he was still really annoyed. I leaned in to kiss him and he immediately turned away. "Don't kiss me right now," he said.

I paused in a state of shock. *What? Don't kiss my fiancé? Are you crazy?* I thought. But I took a step back, knowing that I didn't want to make him upset.

"How did your race go?" I asked.

"It was fine," he replied. "I'm going home."

"Do you want me to come over?" I questioned.

"No." He turned on his heel and walked away.

I stood there for a moment fiddling with my engagement ring, then walked the other direction back towards my car.

*This is going to end,* I thought. *Today, this is going to end. I can feel it.*

I drove home in a daze.

*What is happening to the perfect life I had envisioned?* I asked myself as I drove home. Ever since I was a little girl, I had dreamt of a love story with a man who loved me and a marriage that would last forever. After all, my parents were still married after 38 years, they had met on my Mom's family farm and worked together running our farm. I always imagined I would have a strong marriage like theirs without many issues. When did everything go so awry? I knew things hadn't been perfect, but I didn't understand where I had gone wrong, because surely this whole thing was my fault. I blamed myself for everything at this point.

I arrived home and took a shower. While I was getting ready, my fiancé texted me and asked me to come over. I had a bad feeling the moment my phone chimed, but I agreed to come by in an hour or so. I ate some food and headed to his house.

It was early afternoon when I arrived. I parked in the driveway and walked to the front door. I cautiously walked in to find him sitting on the couch waiting for me.

"Come sit down," he said. "We need to talk."

I carefully sat down a few feet away from him on the couch, turning my body to face him.

"This isn't working," he started. "It's just not. And I don't want to do it anymore."

"What do you mean?" I asked as I fiddled with my engagement ring again.

"I mean I don't want to marry you. I don't want to be engaged. This isn't working."

"What??" I asked slowly as tears began to well up in my eyes. "Are you serious right now?"

"Yes. Very serious," he said gently. I'm sure he could feel my heart shattering into a million pieces as he stated those words.

I began to cry. I began to beg. I began to sob into my hands. He didn't touch me. He told me he was sorry but that he couldn't do it anymore. I continued to beg for him to reconsider.

"You can't be serious," I cried. "We're meant to be together!"

"Sometimes people think they are meant to be together, but they aren't," he responded. I couldn't believe how honest he was in the moment.

I continued to cry and beg him to change his mind.

"What do I tell everyone?" I sobbed.

"The same thing I will tell everyone. It just wasn't right, and we are going our separate ways."

It felt like I was having a business conversation with the man that I loved. He was sensitive, but not supportive. He had been finished for days before that, I'm sure. It became painfully obvious that he had formulated what to say to me, as if he could soften the incredible blow when he pulled the rug out from under me.

I continued to sob, but I knew nothing I did would help. It was done. For real this time. There was no repairing a broken engagement.

"You know you can't get me back like all the times before, right?" I said with defiance. "If you try to come back, you need to know this is done and you can't change my mind."

"Yes, I know," he said quietly.

Nearly an hour had passed of talking, pleading, crying and discussing all the things that were broken in our relationship. All the ways things didn't work along with some of the ways they did.

Then I asked, "What do you want to do with my ring?"

"We can put it in the safe." He got up and headed towards the safe in the other room. I reluctantly followed him, still wiping tears from my eyes.

"Do you want to put it inside?" he asked.

"No," I replied coldly as I took the ring off and placed it in his hand. He put the ring in the box it came in and closed the door, spinning the lock.

It was done. The relationship I had fought for time and time again was over. What was I going to tell everyone? What was I going to do? I went to his room and grabbed the things I had left there to take home with me. I didn't want to come back. I didn't want this to hurt as badly as it was, but I couldn't stop it. I just knew I needed to get out of the house.

After I gathered my things, he walked me to the door and gave me a hug. I hugged him back and began crying again. We said goodbye and I walked out the door in a flood of tears. I got in my car and immediately called Kelly.

"Kel, he called it off. He took the ring. It's over," I sobbed.

"Oh my gosh, come over," she replied. Kelly lived nearby, so I drove straight there. She greeted me with a hug as her boyfriend at the time started baking brownies for the poor girl who had just been shattered.

I spent the next five or six hours on Kelly's couch, crying off and on. Replaying our relationship – and our breakup – over and over in my head. Talking through all the things I thought I could have changed. Trying to understand why my life just flipped upside down. I didn't know what to do.

I couldn't call my parents. First, I was afraid my Dad would go after him. Second, how do you tell your parents that the wedding is off when they've already forked out several thousand dollars for your wedding? I knew that I needed to tell them in person.

Around 9 p.m. I headed home. I crawled in bed and set my alarm for 5:30 a.m. so I could get up early to get to work. I wanted to get in around 7 a.m., get all my emails done and make a list of things for my coworker Rachel to handle while I was out. I was going to drive to Durham to spend time with my family after I told my boss what had happened. I don't remember if I slept that night, but my guess is that it was very restless.

The next morning I woke up at 5:30 a.m., took a shower and made some breakfast. I didn't want to eat but I knew I had to if I were going to function at all that day. I kept moving around the house and packed my things for my parent's house. Staying busy helped me to not remember what had happened the day before. I left for work at 6:30 a.m. The drive to work was brutal. I fought back tears so many times and tried to focus on the things I needed to get done. When I arrived at the office, I was the only one there.

*Thank goodness*, I thought. *I can't handle being around anyone right now.* I opened my computer and started going through my emails. I wrote out a list of things I needed Rachel to cover and started forwarding her emails.

At 7:30 a.m. my co-worker Heidi walked in. She sat in the office directly across the hallway from me so we could see each other. When she sat down I took a deep breath and slowly stood up and walked towards her. I stopped outside her office.

"Hey! You're here early," Heidi said.

"Yeah," I said shakily. She immediately knew something was wrong.

With a quivering lip I said, "Can I talk to you?"

"Of course," she said as she came around her desk and sat me in a chair by her door. "What happened?"

"My fiancé called it off last night. Called off our engagement," I said through tears streaming down my cheeks.

Heidi knelt in front of me and just hugged me telling me how sorry she was. I sat there and cried, then asked her if I could stay in her office until our boss Sarah came in. She let me, of course, and got me some Kleenex.

I went on to tell Heidi what happened and she kept telling me how sorry she was. What do you really say to someone when that happens? It's soul crushing.

Around 8 a.m. Sarah came in and went straight to her office next to mine. I looked at Heidi, almost asking her to come into Sarah's office with me. She instinctively got up and walked me over.

Sarah could tell something was terribly wrong when I walked in with red puffy eyes and Heidi guiding me with a hand on my back. Heidi and I both sat in the chairs opposite Sarah at her desk.

"What's going on?" Sarah said concerned.

"My fiancé called off our engagement last night," I said, unable to get anything else out before the tears came again.

Sarah stood immediately and came around her desk to hug me. I cried for a few minutes as she sat back down.

"I'm going to take today and tomorrow off, if that's OK?" I asked.

"Of course. Whatever you need," Sarah replied.

"I'm going to go back to home to see my family. I've already forwarded all work to Rachel and she will be able to take care of it for me. I'll have my computer too." I started spouting things off so fast, trying to show Sarah I wouldn't let my work slide.

"Laura," she said calmly. "It's OK. Take care of yourself. We will handle things here."

"Thank you," I replied. "I'm just…" but I couldn't get anything else out.

Heidi walked me back to my office. Rachel had come in, so I gathered my things and went to her desk to give her the list of projects to handle. I quickly told her what happened, asked her to cover for me and walked out of the office. I couldn't handle being there one more minute.

The flood of tears started as I left the building. I stepped out into the sunshine on the sidewalk and couldn't help but feel that God was punishing me for something I had done wrong in my life. *Why would God do this to me? Why would I be put in such an awful and heart-wrenching situation?*

As I walked the few blocks to my car, I thought back to when I saw Sex and the City: The Movie in the theater shortly before meeting my now ex-fiancé. When Carrie was left at the altar by Big, I remember thinking, *If that ever happens to me, I hope my friends are there for me like they were for her.* I knew they would be, but that walk to my car was the loneliest I had felt in a very long time.

I drove the two hours back to my childhood home. I pulled in the driveway and my Mom immediately walked out the back door with a look of concern on her face. I got out of the car and just started sobbing.

"Honey, what happened?" Mom asked, obviously alarmed.

"He called it off Mom. He took the ring. It's over," I said between sobs.

My Mom wrapped me up in the biggest hug I've ever felt and told me it was OK. As I collapsed in her arms all I could say to her was I'm sorry over and over again. I felt so guilty they had already forked out money for a wedding that wasn't going to happen. I felt like I had failed them because I couldn't make the fairytale work. I didn't want to have this blemish on my life record. A broken engagement. Something I never imagined in my life plan. It was the most awful feeling of failure I had ever experienced.

I spent the next few days at my parents' farm before heading home to resume my normal life. My friends called and texted constantly. Kelly talked to me every day. One of my good guy friend's called or texted me every single day for two months to make sure I was still functioning. My girlfriends at work constantly checked in with me. My friends from back home were calling and texting daily. They were there for me, just like Carrie's friends were there for her. When my world crumbled down around me, they were there.

The next year was a very dark time in my life. I had never felt as down and depressed as I did in the months after we broke up. Even more than that, I wasn't myself. I fell into a habit of drinking too much, partying constantly and spending money because I felt I was entitled to. Luckily I didn't let my workouts and running slide. I continued to put my heart into what I loved and plugged forward towards all the goals I had set, including running an ultramarathon.

Over time, I realized that loving someone is never wrong because it will always teach you a lesson. It will teach you that you are worthy of the best. It will teach you that through storms come rainbows and you will always come out of the rain. It taught me that while I felt so incredibly alone, I wasn't – I was surrounded by friends and family who loved me very much. It also taught me that sometimes relationships are really hard. But they are usually worth fighting for. And in some cases, giving up the fight is the healthiest thing for everyone involved.

I don't regret my relationship with my ex-fiancé. It led me to so many amazing things in my life and so many amazing people. I still have some great friends I met through our relationship. As I look back on the situation I smile, knowing that things are exactly as they were meant to be.

# FIVE

## Saturday, June 27, 2015 – Mile 16 - 9:40 a.m.

I slowly jogged along the trail as I finished my Oreos. I took several swigs of Skratch and decided to walk for a bit. It was about eight miles to Duncan Canyon and another six up to Robinson Flat, where I would get to see my crew.

*Oh my goodness I can't wait to see them,* I thought to myself.

I was tired. I was beat already. I felt so depleted no matter how much I ate or drank. I just wanted to be out of the altitude so I could breathe normally. My mental status was fleeting the further I got behind the 30-hour time.

*How am I going to do this?*

"You're going to keep putting one foot in front of the other," I said out loud to myself, knowing I probably sounded like a crazy person to anyone who heard me.

I picked up my walking pace trying to give my legs a little rest from running, but still making time. I pumped my arms to push my legs a little faster and kept my head up as I moved along the trail. My shoulders were relaxed allowing me to relax into my momentum more. My mind wandered to all kinds of places. And then I remembered.

"Oh my gosh, Rich works the next aid station!" I picked up my pace to a jog. Rich and I had met through Instagram the year before when we both ran the American River 50 Mile Endurance Run. We met up later that year when we went to Arizona to both run the Javelina Jundred as our qualifier for Western States. He had arrived at the race by himself, but his wife and friend surprised him when they flew in and showed up at the race. Before they arrived, he hung out with my crew and me as we prepped for the race.

At Javelina Jundred in November 2014, you ran clockwise and counterclockwise loops seven times to get to 100 miles for the race. Rich was much faster than me, but we made sure to give each other a hug and encouragement every time we crossed paths during the race. Each loop I couldn't wait to see him and get a hug from someone I knew. After I finished the race, we messaged each other and Rich told me he would see me at Western States. He would be at the Duncan Canyon aid station with the Quicksilver Running Club. I made a mental note about this so I could look forward to seeing someone I knew.

The trail continued to follow the top of the ridge for a bit, and then slowly started coming down from altitude. Up to that point the terrain had still been spotted with trees and barren in many areas, which made the increasing heat more intense. The views were still amazing as I continued running across the ridge, but I looked forward to finding more shaded areas as I moved along. I could feel the sun on my shoulders and, in my head, thanked Carol for reminding me to put on a little sunscreen before I left the condo that morning. I had run so much in the sun, that my skin was a golden brown already, but the sun in the mountains was always more intense than I remembered.

I checked my watch and knew I was getting close to the cutoff for Duncan Canyon.

"Where is the downhill?" I asked myself. "Why am I not there yet? This sucks!" The race was really taking a toll on me mentally at this point. I kept trying to do the math, but I just couldn't string the times together in my brain. I don't consider myself good at math in general, but add in running and I'm horrible. I finally gave up trying to calculate and decided to just leave it all out there. I needed to move fast to get to the aid station in time.

I came across a photographer a short distance before Duncan Canyon. I recognized him as Hugh, one of the runners from our Fleet Feet Sacramento Trail Training Program. He pretty much popped up out of nowhere on top of the ridge and scared me, as I wasn't expecting to see another human out there. Despite the fright, it was nice to see an actual person as I was struggling pretty bad at this time. I was trying to move fast but was all out of sorts. I smiled and acted silly for a photo.

"Fight On Trojans!" Hugh yelled at me as he held up two fingers.

"Fight On!" I yelled back. He and I were USC fans and always greeted each other with a Victory V when we were at events or runs.

"Do you want my hat?" he asked, pointing at the USC hat on his head.

"I love it, but I'm good in this cooling hat. Thank you!" I responded with a smile as I moved on along the trail. I knew I wasn't making up time, but I took advantage of the slight downhill to get moving a bit.

I looked at my watch and knew I was finally getting close to the Duncan Canyon aid station. The trail went into some heavily wooded areas, which brought welcomed shade as I picked up the pace. Although the ground was less rocky, it was covered in a good amount of pine needles leaving it a bit slippery, and I had to be careful with my footing. I took advantage of the shade and picked up my downhill pace even more.

As I pitter-pattered down the trail I started to wonder how I would find Rich at the aid station or how he would find me. And that's when I saw him.

"Rich!" I screamed as I tore down the trail.

"Laura!" He yelled back. He had a walkie talkie in his hand and quickly spoke into it. "We have runner 1-2-6 coming, runner 1-2-6."

I ran directly into a hug from him. "I am so happy to see you!"

He hugged me back. "You're doing great but you don't have much time, get down to the aid station."

"How far is it?" I asked as I stepped away.

"Just a little ways down this hill. Keep kicking ass!" He yelled as I turned and started running down the hill.

"I will!" I screamed back. It felt so good to see someone I knew!

Then I heard the aid station. It got loud really fast and all of a sudden I was turning the corner into Duncan Canyon aid.

It was pandemonium down there. As I ran in, the aid station volunteers started yelling, "Crew for 1-2-6! Crew for 1-2-6!"

I yelled back, "I don't have crew here!" And I was suddenly surrounded by seven volunteers.

"What do you need?" they asked quickly. I had gone through both of my bottles of Skratch at that point and a good amount of my food.

"Both of these bottles filled with ice water and one pouch of the powder in the zipper pockets."

"I got it," one of the volunteers yelled as she ran off with my bottles.

"You have 12 minutes to get out of here and we are going to move you fast. What else do you need?" one of the volunteers asked.

*Wait, I have 12 minutes to get out of here? What do you mean?* I thought. I glanced at my watch and realized that I was just a few minutes from the 12 p.m. cutoff for Duncan Canyon.

*Is it going to be like this all day?* I thought. *This is brutal!*

"Miss, what else do you need?" another volunteer asked urgently as I hadn't responded.

I quickly checked the front pockets of my pack. "Can you get me a few Vanilla Clif Shots, some Clif Bloks and some pretzels?"

"You got it!"

The volunteer with my bottles came back with everything prepped. Another volunteer took ice cold sponges and squeezed the water over my cooling arm sleeves, as another took my hat off and dunked it in ice cold water. One more volunteer grabbed my neck cooler and put it in the cold water.

"Can one of you dump ice in my sports bra?" I asked.

A woman holding a pitcher of ice responded, "Sure, lean over here." I pulled my tank top and sports bra forward as she proceeded to dump freezing cold ice inside.

"Woooo!" I yelled, laughing. "That's cold!" It was the first time all day I had added ice to my sports bra. My coach, Mo, had instructed me that I was to put ice in my sports bra as many times as I could once it got warm. I had done this the entire race at Javelina

Jundred and several other warm ultras and it had saved me. The ice kept my core cool allowing my body to stay cooler in the high temps.

The temperature that day was supposed to be in the 90s, and a bit humid. And at 90 degrees, the canyons of the course often reached temperatures above 100 degrees. Ice was essential for staying cool and moving forward.

The aid station had a speaker system with music playing and an announcer keeping everyone excited and amped. "This runner has a NASCAR pit crew going over here! Great job volunteers!" he yelled into the microphone as the volunteers continued getting me ready to leave the aid station.

They returned with the food items I had asked for, tucked them in my front pockets handed me my handheld water bottles and told me to get out of the aid station.

"You only have a few minutes. Go now!" they urged.

I looked at them all, paused and said, "Thank you so much. You are amazing."

They patted me on the back and literally pushed me down the trail and out of the aid station.

I took off at an easy trot as the terrain was a steep downhill to start. That's when I realized it. I could breathe. I took a few nice deep breaths and smiled knowing that the worst was behind me and I was now at an altitude my lungs could tolerate.

*Phew*, I thought. *That's a relief.*

Then I thought, *How in the world did I only have 12 minutes to get out of that aid station? Am I not making up any time?*

I came into Duncan Canyon at 6:48 on the race clock, which was 11:48 a.m. The cutoff for Duncan Canyon was 12 p.m. and the 30-hour time was 11:05 a.m. I was now 43 minutes behind the 30-hour time. I had gone from 27 minutes behind to 43 in eight miles. I was slowly watching my race slip through my fingers and I began to get really scared.

As I ran along, taking full advantage of the downhill, I noticed that my feet were starting to feel really warm. *I hope there's a creek along here somewhere* I thought. I loved to get my feet wet in all the water along the course. I was lucky that my feet didn't blister easily so water was my friend later in trail races.

Then I came up on a familiar face. One of the Fleet Feet Sacramento coaches, Joe, was running Safety Patrol that day and was making his way down into Duncan Canyon. I caught up to him and he let me pass. We ran together and chatted for a bit and he took a photo of me. I was all smiles at that point.

The trail continued to descend down into the canyon until we reached Duncan Creek, the first large creek crossing of the race. This year the water wasn't very high, just below my knees in the deepest parts and only about 20 feet across. I took it slow so I could let my feet really soak since they were starting to feel hot. That's when I left Joe and started hiking up to Robinson Flat.

*What is this uphill?* I thought. *This can't be too long.*

I hadn't realized that Duncan Canyon actually meant that it was a canyon. I should have known, but I had never been on the course above Robinson Flat so this was all new to me. I started the ascent up to Robinson Flat at a strong pace. Marching up the hill I started going over the course in my head.

*Where am I? Where is my crew? How many miles to Robinson? Turn it on, Laura. Good form. Hike with power. Use your glutes.*

The terrain was rocky, much like the first section of the race. There were many more trees along the course, along with shrubbery and ground cover. By this time the sun was blazing overhead and I was feeling hot. I had done a good job of keeping my arm sleeves wet and my neck band iced, but they were already dried out in just the few miles since Duncan Canyon aid.

*I should have gotten my sleeves wet again in the creek,* I scolded myself. Luckily there was still plenty of ice in my sports bra keeping me a bit cool.

I pulled a Clif Shot gel out of my pocket and ate it quickly to give me some extra energy as I continued up the hill. I practiced my uphill walking just like I had done in my months of training. *Keep putting one foot in front of the other,* I thought. *Keep marching forward. You got this. Breathe in, breathe out.*

Then I came across the first runner sitting on the side of the trail. He had found a small patch of shade and was sitting on the ground. I asked if he was OK and he responded with a weary yes and I kept moving by. One thing I knew I couldn't do was try to help someone else if they were responsive. I wasn't going to leave someone in distress on the course, but I had to keep moving to complete this race. Plus, I knew that there were so many safety patrol runners and sweepers that no one would be left behind out there.

That runner was my first experience with the carnage that would come in this race. I came across four or five other runners on the climb. They were all in the same position, sitting or kneeling on the ground. A few were getting sick. One told me he just needed to rest. I trudged on after telling them to keep moving and that we were almost there, but at that point I didn't even know if I was going to make it to Robinson Flat.

I started to think about Dusty and Pat, the general manager and owner of Fleet Feet Sacramento. That's where I worked at the time, not only selling shoes and merchandise, but also handling marketing for the store, events and training programs. Each year, Fleet Feet Sacramento received a spot in the race for one person. This was because of their management of the Ford's Bar aid station at Mile 73 of the race. Fleet Feet Sacramento chose someone based on several criteria, including the need to have a qualifying race before the lottery date.

That year, Bob and I were the only two employees vying for the spot. We were both going to run the Javelina Jundred as our qualifier so we could be considered. Before Javelina Jundred, Bob came up to me and told me he had decided not to run the race and qualify for Western States that year. I looked at him inquisitively as he said, "So I need you to go and get that Western States spot, OK?"

My mouth dropped open. Had Bob just told me he wasn't going to qualify for States that year? Was the door just opened for me to be the ONLY qualifier vying for the spot? I smiled at him and said, "I will! Thanks Bob!" And he smiled and walked away. My mouth hung open for a moment as I let that sink in.

In November 2014, I traveled to McDowell Mountain Regional Park in Arizona and ran my first 100-mile race, finishing in 28 hours and 10 minutes. After I received my buckle and took a few photos with my pacers and crew, I sent a text to then Fleet Feet Sacramento owners Pat and Jan, showing them that I had finished.

Jan texted back, "Next up is Western States!" I almost passed out when I saw that message. I was in! It was real and I was running States. What a dream come true!

The day before I left for Western States, I was talking to Pat and Dusty in their office. They both jokingly said to me, "We're looking forward to you bringing home a buckle. We need another finisher!"

"I'm coming home with a buckle! Don't worry!" I replied confidently.

While hiking up towards Robinson Flat I started to think *What am I going to tell Pat and Dusty if I don't finish? What will I tell them? I can't fail them!*

I kept pushing and putting one foot in front of the other. That's when I noticed it. My breathing had become much more labored again.

*What is happening to me?* I thought. My lungs just couldn't fill with air. I was almost gasping as I tried to keep moving forward.

"Am I back at altitude?" I questioned. The Robinson Flat aid station is at approximately 6,700 feet of altitude. On my climb back up I passed 6,500 feet and that's when I really started to feel the altitude on my lungs again. My pace slowed, and it was so difficult to find momentum. I had no idea where the top of the mountain was, but then I saw someone coming towards me down the trail.

*That's a good sign,* I thought. *I must be coming up on the aid station if someone is coming this direction looking for a runner.* It turns out I was only a mile from Robinson Flat. Soon the course flattened out and I was able to run a bit as I came up the trail around the small meadow towards the aid station. That's when I saw my friend Paul taking photos.

"You look good Laura. The aid station is right around the corner," Paul said.

I gave him a weak grin and kept running. After checking my watch on the way up the hill I knew that I was really close to not making it out of the aid station in time.

Then I heard him. "Laura! Come this way!" It was my crew member Andy. He had run around the aid station to the other side to greet me. "Just keep running, you got this. We're on the other side of the aid station," he said. I followed him down the gravel path and into the aid station as he made his way around it. Crews were not allowed into aid station nutrition areas, even to fill water bottles. In order to keep crowds under control, only runners and pacers with actual pacer bibs on were allowed to enter the nutrition areas. I went straight for the water table and handed my bottles over to the volunteers, asking them to make my Skratch. As they took my bottles, I leaned over on the large water jugs on the table to catch my breath.

The volunteers behind the table stood there wide-eyed for a few moments. "You have about 10 minutes to get out of the aid station before the cutoff."

"What?" I said. They repeated what they had said and in a blur I took my full bottles from them and made my way out of the other side of the aid station where Andy was waiting for me. We ran down to the end of the path past other crews waiting for their runners to come in.

My crew had set up right before the bridge at the end of the aid station. This was the spot where they checked runners out of the aid station. The time they recorded was the time that counted on the clock. I had to make it past the person checking off my bib at the end of the bridge by the cutoff to still be in the race.

That's when the horn sounded. One air horn blast. At the aid stations where there are strict cutoffs, there is a horn sounding that happens at 30, 20 and 10 minutes to cutoff. Three blasts for 30, two blasts for 20 and one blast for 10. The 10-minute blast had just happened.

"How do I only have 10 minutes?" I asked my crew.

"It's been a rough day. You're doing fine. We're going to get you out of here," they responded.

I stood there like a zombie as Carol pulled the trash out of my pack and Joe added more packs of Skratch powder to my handhelds. They stuffed my pockets with more fuel and took off my hat. Carol had my cooling hat ready and iced down for me to put on. This hat had a white drape on the back to keep my neck cool as I went into the hottest part of the day.

"You look pale, are you eating and drinking?" Carol asked, concerned.

"I am. That was a brutal climb," I replied. "Honestly, I feel like shit."

"Well you've got this, so get it done girl," she ordered.

"I don't have time to change my shoes and socks, but I wish I could," I told Carol.

"I know you do, but you're right, there's no time."

Andy started rattling off numbers and times to me, letting me know that I was behind schedule, but to just keep moving forward and I would be OK. I looked at each of them, concern painted on their faces. They didn't think I was going to make it. I could tell. I was exhausted. I was beat down. I was fearful of the outcome of this day. This was the hardest thing I had ever done in my life, and I was going to fail.

"How far behind am I now?" I asked.

Andy slowly responded, "You're getting out of here now with 7 minutes left before cutoff. But you are 48 minutes behind the 30-hour time now."

I was 48 minutes behind. I had lost 5 more minutes in the time between Duncan Canyon and Robinson Flat. This race was tearing me apart.

I looked up at my three crew members all staring at me. "I don't know if I will finish this guys."

"You're doing fine, Laura," Carol said as she handed me a pack of Honey Stinger chews. "You got this." But we all knew what may happen.

I strapped my bottles on my hands, kissed Joe goodbye and started walking across the bridge out of the aid station. "Thank you guys!" I called back to my crew.

"1-2-6 out," I said to the person checking us out of the aid station.

"Thank you," they responded.

I knew full well that the next time my crew saw me at the race, they would most likely be picking me up somewhere along the course when I dropped. I didn't want to see my dreams dashed, but this course was far more than I thought it would be. It had pushed my body harder than I imagined it would.

I was slowly coming to terms with this being the end of the road for my Western States dreams.

# SIX
## January 29, 2013

It was a chilly, January day in Sacramento and I was at work going through my emails. My co-workers were slowly filing into their offices to start their days. I saw my boss, Sarah, walk past my office towards the conference room. About 15 minutes later, Danielle came by my desk and asked me to come to the conference room.

*That's strange,* I thought. Danielle never called me to meetings. *Must be an impromptu meeting. Or maybe a new proposal request came out.* I grabbed a yellow ledger pad and a pen and headed to the conference room.

Our conference room was a like fishbowl with glass windows on the side where our offices were. I could see that the room had several people sitting in it so I hustled around the corner and to the door. That's when I saw Julia sitting across the table from the doorway. I stopped in my tracks. Julia was our accountant and human resources manager. I glanced to my left and saw my co-worker Scott staring back at me, wide-eyed. I knew exactly what was happening. I was being laid off.

I slowly walked to the empty seat next to Scott and sat down as the tears welled up in my eyes. Scott looked at me. I don't know that he realized what was happening.

I glanced up at Sarah as she said, "I think you know why we're here."

"Yes, I do," I replied. About a month ago, we had re-pitched two accounts I managed. Both were up for re-bid in Fall/Winter and we unfortunately lost them both to other firms in town.

The minute we found out that we had lost both accounts, I knew my days working at my company were numbered. I had even told my friend Chris that I would be laid off if I wasn't able to help us get some more accounts for me to manage. I understood that being laid off wasn't a result of anything I had done, just as it wasn't a reflection of my bosses or our management team. It was plain and simple – if there's no work to give you, there's no job for you. I know we all fought to find more work and more proposals to pitch, but you can only do that for so long, then you have to make business decisions.

I peered across the table at Holly, who looked as if she may start crying.

Sarah continued, "Scott. Laura. Today is your last day here. This has nothing to do with either of you personally. You both just worked almost exclusively on the accounts we no longer have and we had to make some really tough decisions."

I managed a half smile at Sarah as tears filled my eyes and began to run over. "It's OK," I replied quietly. "I knew this would happen if we didn't secure a few more large accounts. It's not your fault, guys."

Then Michael spoke up. "We think you are both incredible people and very hard workers. We will help you both get on your feet and find something else. Whatever you need. We don't want you to feel abandoned."

"Thanks Michael," I replied. "We really appreciate it."

"I'm so sorry, you guys," Holly offered. She seemed to be taking it really hard. I offered her a weak smile, knowing there was nothing they could do.

"I have your final checks here. I also have a severance for each of you that will hopefully cover the time you are unemployed," Julia said. "We've also cut checks for the paid time off you had accrued at this point." She slid two stacks of envelopes across the table to each of us.

We gently took the checks and held them in our trembling hands as we blinked back tears. I looked at Scott and offered a weak smile and he stared back at me, still wide-eyed.

I swallowed hard to fight tears. "So, what's next?"

"Here is also some information on unemployment with the state," Julia replied. "I recommend that you go online right away and get your information put in. It can take a few weeks to get your first check, but you are both entitled to unemployment funds."

"OK, thanks," I replied as Julia pushed the other paperwork across the table.

I swallowed again. "I want to thank you all for the opportunity to have worked with you for the past few years. I have had some of my best times here and appreciate all you've taught me and offered to me."

"Yeah," Scott spoke up. "Thank you so much. I'm really sad, but I understand," he said as he looked down at his hands.

"We will walk you back to your desks to get your things and will walk you out where we will take your keys and key cards," Julia said. "It's nothing against you guys. It's just procedure."

"I completely understand," I replied. I slowly pushed back from the table and stood up. Michael was sitting closest to me and offered a big hug.

"You'll be back on your feet in no time," he said.

"Thanks," I responded.

Sarah stepped towards me. "Thank you for working hard for us. And really, if you need anything, I'm happy to help however I can." She gave me a warm hug, similar to the day I told her my ex-fiancé had called off our engagement.

Julia gave me a hug and a small smile. She knows how hard it is to let employees go since she's always involved. Holly hugged me as left the conference room and escorted Scott back to his desk.

Danielle walked over to me. "I'll take you to your office," she said.

We walked back to my office and I sat to shut down my computer. When I saw the screen, I knew I wouldn't even need to do that. They had shut it down and logged me out already through our IT team. I know it is protocol to do things like that, but it was like another dagger through the heart.

I remember thinking, *man, that's harsh.*

I gathered my purse and a few personal things. "When can I get the rest of my stuff?" I asked Danielle.

"Julia will call you later to set up a time when you can come by and clear out your office. We won't do anything to it, don't worry."

"I know you won't. OK, I'll chat with Julia later."

We walked out of my office and Danielle led me towards the elevator. Scott was already on his way out of the building as we headed down to the bottom floor. Danielle walked me to the glass door leading to the street and outstretched her hand.

"My garage key card is in my car. Can I give that to Julia when I come back to get my things?" I asked.

"Of course you can. No worries."

I gently placed my office key card and office key in her hand. She reached out and gave me a big hug.

"Really, Laura. If you need any help, we will write letters of recommendation or whatever you need. It was really great to work with you," Danielle said as she placed her hand on my shoulder.

"Thank you," I said. "I really do appreciate it." I pushed the door open and walked into the parking lot, and towards the bustling street.

*Did that just happen? Wow. This is awful.* I continued walking and made the right-hand turn towards my car parked a block down the street. I saw Scott walking in front of me about 30 yards ahead.

"Scott!" I yelled after him and started at a little jog down the street. "Hey," he replied. He had been walking with his head dropped and had a look of disbelief on his face.

"Did that really just happen?" he asked me.

"Yeah, it did. I knew it would eventually, but I still wasn't expecting it," I replied sadly.

"I didn't think it would happen," he said slowly.

I gave him a hug. "It will be OK Scott. I know we don't feel like it right now, but it will. You gonna be OK?"

"Yeah," he said. "I'm just gonna head home."

"OK. Call or text me if you need anything," I said.

We parted ways at the next intersection. Scott headed towards the parking structure while I crossed the street to go to my car parked down the way. That's when I started crying. I pulled my phone out of my pocket and dialed my boyfriend. I got his voicemail and left a desperate message.

"Babe. I just got laid off! Why aren't you answering your phone?!" I cried into the phone.

I was an emotional mess. *How did this happen? What am I going to do?* I thought. I had so many bills to pay and I couldn't afford them all without a job. I felt lost and alone.

I felt like a failure. What I didn't know was that this would lead me into a whole different direction for my life.

I reached my car parked and unlocked it. Sliding into the front seat, I tossed my purse and the few things I had taken with me on the passenger seat and just sat there, staring at the steering wheel.

*What do I do now?* I thought.

I texted my close friends Chris and Megan first.

"Just got laid off. Awesome," I wrote in a group text. Almost immediately Megan responded, "WHAT? I just saw you."

"I know. I'm in my car now. I'm heading home. They escorted Scott and me out."

"OH MY GOSH!" she replied.

Chris chimed in, "You're kidding, right?"

"No, I'm not," I said back, being short with him.

I sent another text. "Apparently Julia will contact me for a time I can come back and get my things. Probably tomorrow."

"Can we do anything for you?" Megan asked.

"No. I just want to go home. I'll chat with you both later," I said. I was over being in town. Over being near "work." Over it all.

I started my car and pulled onto the street to head for the freeway. Tears welled in my eyes and the waterworks started as I made the left at the first light.

"Get yourself together, Laura. You need to drive home safely," I said out loud.

I gripped the wheel with both hands, blinked back the tears and made a right at the next light towards the freeway onramp.

◆ ◆ ◆

After a few days being home, I started to feel a bit better. I had filed my paperwork for unemployment and hoped to have those checks coming in sooner than later. I had a roommate, so that helped with the mortgage on my condo for the time being. And the stipend they had provided, along with my paid time off check, was going to keep me afloat for several weeks.

I started job searching but nothing was striking my interest. Maybe because I was so close to my layoff. Maybe because I wasn't feeling the career anymore. I wasn't sure. I continued to put my resume out there. I reached out to contacts I had from previous jobs and my work with the AAF Sacramento Ad Club to hopefully stir up some leads. I had a phone interview with a winery for a marketing job, but wasn't a fit for the position. I found myself fumbling through trying to get another advertising agency job.

Maybe I really didn't want one.

I was ready for a break from agency life. I had been working in public relations, advertising and marketing at agencies for the past nine years and was burnt out. I was ready for a change. I decided that I would accept an in-house position at a company if it was a real fit for me, but I wasn't going to sell myself short to do something I really wasn't committed to.

A little over a week into my search I started to get worried about not having a job. I'm a worker. I like to work. I like to stay busy. I like to be around people and be social. Sitting at home with my dog wasn't really tickling my fancy, per se.

Years before, I had been told that I would be a good massage therapist. There had been a few occasions when friends would have sore shoulders and I'd offer to work on them. It was something I had always enjoyed doing and I knew how helpful massage had been for me in my experience running.

"What if I went back to school?" I asked myself. "What if I became a massage therapist?" Was this a crazy idea? At the time, probably. But would it make me happy? Sure!

I sat down on my couch, opened my laptop and started researching how to become a massage therapist. I found all kinds of information, as well as different schools I could attend. I bookmarked pages, started looking at costs and made a mental note to talk to my Mom about it when I headed back home that weekend.

That Friday I was sitting on the couch at my parents' house and told my Mom I was thinking of going back to school to become a massage therapist.

"OK," my Mom said. "How long will that take?"

"The program I'm looking at is in Sacramento at Bryan College. It's a part of Bryan University out of Arizona," I told her. "It looks like it's a 15-month program, but you come out of it certified and with an Associates degree which would be pretty cool!"

"Great!" she said. "Will you take out a loan?"

"Yeah, I figure that will be easiest. Then I'll just pay it off when I'm out of school and back working."

"Sounds like you have a plan then."

I went online and made an appointment to meet with an advisor at the school the next week.

◆◆◆

I arrived at Bryan College early in the morning on February 11, before classes started. I was excited to see if I liked the school and to decide if this is what I wanted to do with my life. The advisor greeted me in the lobby and took me back to her office.

"So, you want to pursue massage therapy? When did you want to start?" she asked. I didn't know it at the time, but the next group of students were starting that very morning and were in class at 8 a.m. "I don't want to pressure you, but we start our modules every 5 weeks and the next one is actually starting this morning."

"Oh! It is?" I asked. "I don't know if I'm ready to start this morning. I haven't even figured out the cost or anything."

"How about this? I'll give you a quick tour of our campus, then you can sit in on the first few hours, see if you like it and come back to see me when they start the hands on portion of class," she offered. "If you hate it, we will part ways. If you love it, I will get you enrolled, you can talk to financial aid and we will have you set to go before you leave here."

"Wow! You'll do that?" I asked.

"Sure! From your email you seem really interested and I'd hate to make you miss this start date and have to wait five weeks for the next one."

"Well, OK! Why not?" I replied.

"Great," the advisor said. "I'm sure you don't have any note paper or anything so let me lend you a notepad and pen, then you can take notes if needed."

"That would be great, thanks!" I replied.

It was now 8:30 so I had missed the first part of class, but the advisor escorted me down to the classroom, gently knocking on the door.

"Come in?" the instructor replied, in a questioning voice. The advisor opened the door to a dimly lit classroom with about 10 students sitting two-by-two behind massage tables they were using as desks.

"Hi Jane," she said. "This is Laura. She's a late registrant and will be sitting in for this morning's class. Send her back to me when you start the hands on portion."

"OK. Thanks. Laura, you can take a seat there in the second row," she offered as she gestured to the open seat.

"Thank you," I said. "Sorry for the interruption."

"No worries. We're just going over the history of massage therapy."

Jane continued teaching until the first break at 8:50 a.m. "We have a 10-minute break then we will be back to learn more about where this industry began."

When everyone walked out, she came over to my seat and sat on the table in front of me.

"Just a few things you should know," Jane said. "We always wear black pants. They can be yoga pants, dockers, whatever – as long as they are black. And shorts have to be knee length."

"Oh! Sure. I hadn't even been here until this morning, so I didn't know," I said, looking down at my jeans and hooded sweatshirt.

"No worries at all. We also wear Bryan College polo shirts but we're waiting on our next shipment from the embroiderer, so for now please wear a plain black shirt, no logo, cool?"

"Sure," I said making a note on my notepad.

I stayed for the next hour of class and met with the advisor again around 10 a.m.

"I really like the program!" I said to her. "What are the next steps for me to become an official student?"

We filled out paperwork and I met with the financial aid office to get set up with a student loan. I also met with the counselor to get all my books and massage supplies. After I left I went shopping for couple pairs of black pants and a few black shirts. I wanted to be sure I looked the part on my second day.

The first 5-week class module proved to me that I was right where I belonged. I took to massage therapy like a duck to water. I already understood the body and how it worked so moving into the massage space was an easy transition. I aced my first classes and received awards for academic excellence.

In April 2013, I saw a job posting on Facebook for Fleet Feet Sacramento. They were hiring folks to sell shoes at their store. Back when I was working at the ad agency, I had applied for the Marketing Manager position at Fleet Feet Sacramento, but didn't get an interview. Now that I was in school and had no job, I felt that having a retail job would be better than no job at all, so I decided to apply. I got a call to set up an interview with one of the managers.

When I went in for my interview, I ended up sitting down with Dusty, the general manager of the store. We chatted about running and he told me that I didn't get an interview for the marketing manager position because I was overqualified for the job.

At the end of my interview, Pat, the owner of the store at the time, came in and we chatted some more. Then he offered me a job. It was awesome! I was on Cloud 9 and so excited to start a new job somewhere I loved. And what could be better than hanging out with a bunch of runners all day?

I began the job with a training on how to fit shoes including education on biomechanics, injuries and products. Within a month I was working the floor selling running gear, fitting patrons for shoes and helping with events. Soon after that the marketing manager put in her 30-day notice to go back to graduate school. A few days later, Dusty called me into his office and offered me the marketing manager position if I wanted to take it. Of course I said yes!

At that time, I was still in school, and would be for the next year. I worked 40 hours a week at Fleet Feet Sacramento and went to school for 20 hours a week. Once I was certified as a massage therapist about halfway through the program, I began working extra to see clients and make more money. In April 2014, I completed massage therapy school and went to work at Fleet Feet Sacramento full time during the days. I saw massage clients at night and on weekends. I was working 55-65 hours a week, but really enjoying both professions. I was able to grow my business through networks of runners and friends who knew I was a runner and a massage therapist.

My life was finally where I wanted it to be. While I still wasn't making as much as I was at the advertising agency, despite working many more hours, I was so passionate about the direction my life had taken that it didn't matter. Yes, I was in debt. I was paying my bills, but barely. I was running any time that I wasn't working. And I loved every minute of it, even when it was hard.

Losing my job ended up being just what I needed to take a leap of faith with my career. I chose to walk away from an industry I thought I would work in for the rest of my life to pursue something that would help people instead. And, as awful as it seemed, losing my job was just the kick in the butt I needed to make a change and fresh start.

Our lives are full of ups and downs. It's what we choose to do during these moments that shows us what we are made of. Do we sit in the same spot and not aim higher? Do we give up just because we've lost our job or something else bad has happened? Or do we take a leap of faith and see where it leads us?

When you run 100 miles you can't just give up or you'll throw your race out the window. You have to take the things that go wrong and push past them. You have to take the downs and work through them. You have to take your plan and sometimes throw it out the window just to survive. Things get hard and sometimes go so wrong that there is no plan. It's what we do in those moments that shows how tough we are.

In my life, having faith that there is a plan, His plan, and the downs are all part of it has been life changing. While no one wants to experience the downs, I know that God is teaching me a life lesson in every tough situation. In life and sport, you have to choose to reach higher, work harder and live smarter. When things go awry, you have to leave everything out there and take a leap of faith that all will be OK. Finding the things that work and really believing in ourselves is what it takes to reach the finish line.

# SEVEN

## Saturday, June 27, 2015 – Mile 30 - 1:43 p.m.

I slowly walked away from the Robinson Flat aid station carrying a pack of Honey Stinger chews in my fingers. I tore open the package and started eating them because I knew I had gotten behind on my fueling while I was out there. I wasn't sure how it had happened, but I knew I was behind.

*Is this it?* I thought to myself. *Is this all I have left in me? Is this where my States dreams will end?*

I felt crushed. The full weight of the race was falling on me now. I couldn't stop thinking about all the people I would let down. Dusty. Pat. Jan. Everyone at Fleet Feet. My crew. My friends. My family, who didn't even know how big this race was. I was going to let them all down because I was going to fail.

I looked up as I finished eating the chews and tucked the trash in the front pocket of my pack. There was a man walking towards me down the trail. He was smiling this huge, bright smile and said, "You can still make it to Miller's Defeat!"

I smiled weakly at him and asked, "How far is it?"

"4.4 miles and the cutoff is 3 p.m. You can do it!" he said encouragingly.

I glanced at my watch; it was 1:55 p.m. That gave me an hour and five minutes to go four miles. I had to run a 15-minute pace or faster to get there in time… and at this point even moving at an 18-minute pace seemed daunting.

The man was John Trent, the Western States President at the time. He smiled his classic smile and wished me luck as I walked on. *Was this a sign to keep going?*

I tried to wrap my head around where I was going and how long it would take me. I was almost to the highest point heading out of the aid station and as I crested the hill, the view before me was spectacular. You could see for miles and miles over the terrain. It was gorgeous and breathtaking. The mountains rolled like plush little hills as far as the eye could see.

*I am so lucky to see this,* I reflected. *So many people never get to see or do things like this and I get to.*

At that moment I decided this was my last chance to leave everything out there and stay in this race. I knew I could do it, I just had to believe I could do it. I had told my crew from the beginning that the only way I would leave this race before the finish would be if I were pulled due to time or injured. And I wasn't about to let anyone stop me from finishing the race.

I started running downhill following several runners I saw up ahead. I was moving along at a quick pace when I passed the first runner. It was then that I noticed my breathing had become easier. Coming down out of the altitude was helping me keep my pace up.

The ground was really rocky, so I had to be careful how I placed my feet, but I also knew I had to move quickly to make it to Miller's Defeat under time. I passed a few more runners as I proceeded down the trail. Each time I passed a runner, I started going faster. It was like passing them gave me a boost of energy to chase down the next person.

Then I saw a runner up ahead that I had met at a few other ultra events. *Catch him,* I thought to myself as I picked up the pace.

I caught and passed him as the single-track trail merged with the fire road. The trail continued uphill for a short time, and then flattened out. I started running faster as I took on the flat and downhill sections ahead. The dirt road was smooth, so running faster was relatively easy. I kept checking my watch and knew I was getting close to the cutoff for Miller's Defeat, but I couldn't see the aid station.

I looked at my watch again. I had run more than four miles and the aid station was nowhere to be found. I came around a corner where the aid station should have been and stopped in the middle of the trail.

*Where is it?* I thought. *It should be here!* But I couldn't see anything anywhere around me. I walked a few steps trying to catch my breath and then I saw it. Blue tents up ahead around the bend, about 200 yards. I glanced at my watch. I only had a few minutes until the cutoff!

I started running as fast as I could towards the aid station. *Pump your arms and RUN Laura!* I got down to a 7:30 pace as I flew along the dirt road.

About 20 yards from the aid station entrance I started screaming, "Did I make it? Did I make the cutoff?!"

The aid station timer sitting at the entrance yelled, "You have to get in now!"

I sprinted through the entrance like a sprinter crossing a finish line yelling, "1-2-6 IN!"

The timer responded, "You have two minutes to get your stuff and get out!"

I slowed and peered to my left at the aid station volunteers. They were all standing behind the food and fluids tables, with pitchers of water in their hands, wide-eyed and waiting for my instructions. I had one full bottle of Skratch on me, gels in my pocket and only 3.5 miles to the next aid station.

I turned and started running towards the exit yelling, "I don't need anything… 1-2-6 OUT!"

The volunteers screamed and cheered as I shot out the other side of the aid station. "Now that's the way you do it!"

I slowed down once I cleared the other end of the aid station, trying to catch my breath.

*What just happened?* I thought to myself, barely able to breathe. As I began to walk, a volunteer came running up next to me.

"You have 3.5 miles to the next aid station," he said. "You're doing great! Keep it up!"

I smiled and said thank you as I kept walking.

This was it. This was the effort level I was going to have to put in to keep getting through each aid station at this race. I was going to have to prove everything to myself and put all the energy I had out there for the rest of the day.

"I will leave everything out here today," I said out loud. "I will not go down without a fight."

I drank some Skratch and took deep breaths as I thought back to watching Western Time the day before. In the film, when Sally McRae left Green Gate, her first pacer David was interviewed. Through exhaustion and tears he said, "She's gonna do it. She's gonna do it. She ran so hard."

As I continued walking towards the next aid station, I looked up towards the sky and said, "I ran so hard. I am going to do this. I ran SO HARD!"

There was no way I would quit this race. I would leave everything I had out on that course to get a buckle. I would run into every aid station not knowing if I made the cutoff, but knowing I had done everything I could. I reminded myself that telling people I had dropped or been pulled was NOT what I came here to do. I came here to finish this race and take home a buckle.

*I will not let this course take me,* I thought.

I had clocked into Miller's Defeat with three minutes to spare before the cutoff. I was now 42 minutes behind the 30-hour time. I had made up six minutes in the past four miles, but was still pretty far behind the time I needed to finish.

Just then four other runners came up alongside me. *Yay! They had made it too!*

"Hey guys!" I said.

"Man, that was rough," they responded.

"But we made it!" I said. "Let's just keep moving and checking off each aid station. We got this!" I was shocked at my positivity, but I figured if I could keep them positive, it would keep me positive too.

We continued running together down the fire road towards Dusty Corners. It was about 3.5 miles from Miller's Defeat, but mostly flat or downhill terrain on a fire road. The cutoff was at 4:10

pm. So we had 1:10 to get there from when we left Miller's Defeat. I knew we would easily make it. This was also a great place to make up some time on the 30-hour limit.

We stayed pretty close together most of the way to Dusty Corners, talking and sharing about where we were from, how many ultras we had done, and other things to keep our minds off of the running.

We started to hear the aid station chatter as we approached Dusty Corners. There's a long downhill on the fire road as you cross the road to come into Dusty Corners. As I took the sweeping left-hand turn down the hill, I looked up and saw Carol standing about 15 yards in front of me on the side of the trail.

"What are you doing here?" I yelled at her. My crew wasn't supposed to be back at an aid station until Michigan Bluff at mile 55.

"We were worried you didn't have a head lamp," Carol said as we ran down the hill into the aid station together.

Right when I cross the street, my long-time running friend Mike ran up to me, "What do you need?"

"Can you fill both of these bottles with ice water and one pouch each of the powder in the zip pockets?" I asked.

"You got it! I've been waiting for you to come in. I told everyone I got to help you first!" he said back with a smile.

"Awe! Thanks Mike!" I immediately headed for the food table. I grabbed some more Fritos, a couple of Oreos and a few other snacks and walked out of the food area towards my crew.

As I walked up, my team started the aid station routine, like taking my trash and refilling my pack with food. "How on earth did you get here?" I asked with wide eyes.

Anyone who has been a crew member at Western States knows that there are separate routes for Crew A and Crew B. This is because some of the aid stations are on one side of a canyon, while others are on the other side. You can't drive to the aid stations on both sides of the canyon because the distance to drive and the time it takes to get there on foot are so different. This is why I was so shocked to see my crew standing in Dusty Corners, when they weren't slated to be here.

"We knew you were way behind your times so we wanted to be here to bring you a headlamp since you will need it before we see you at Michigan Bluff," Joe said.

"Oh my gosh. Thank you, but I have one in my drop bag at Devil's Thumb," I replied. "How did you guys get here so fast?" I asked as Carol handed me a small bottle of Pepsi.

"Well, Joe drove us here," Andy said. "And I was so scared I took my wallet out of my back pocket and put it in my front pocket. I figured if we went off the cliff at least they could identify my body if my wallet was on me."

"You guys!" I said laughing. "Be safe! But thank you for coming here. I'm so happy to see you."

"Kelly left a little bit ago. She tried to wait to see you," Carol said.

"Awe! Hopefully I'll see her later. How's Todd doing?" I asked as I took a drink of soda. Todd was one of our friends from Sacfit. He was actually running in their sponsor spot that year and Kelly was one of his crew members.

"She said he's doing good. He's on sub 24-hour pace."

"Wow!" I responded, "That's fantastic!" At Western States there are two kinds of buckles you can receive. The first is silver for finishing the 100 miles in less than 24 hours. The other is bronze for those who finish between 24 and 30 hours. Todd had always been a fast runner so I wasn't surprised he was running a sub-24.

"OK, you don't have much time, let's get you out of here," Carol said.

"I'm going to run over to the bathroom really quick," I said, handing Carol my soda.

I took a quick bathroom break and on my way back to my crew, went by the aid station food tents again. I grabbed a few more Oreos from the food table, had the volunteers add more ice in my sports bra and hat and headed back to my crew.

"Take this with you," Carol said handing me a new small Pepsi bottle.

"Thank you. I can definitely use the extra caffeine," I replied as I stuffed the bottle in the front pocket of my pack.

Mike had returned my bottles to my crew while I was in the bathroom and Joe refilled the Skratch powder in the zip pouches. He followed me to the end of the aid station with my bottles in hand.

"I need you to find Brad. Ask him to come to Michigan Bluff instead of Foresthill. I am going to need him there," I said to Joe.

"You got it. I'll get him there," he said as he kissed me and wished me luck. I turned and headed down the wide fire road towards Last Chance.

I came into Dusty Corners at 3:54 p.m. with the cutoff being at 4:10 p.m. I walked out of the aid station at 4:05 p.m. The 30-hour time was 3:15 p.m. I had made up another three minutes in that section, putting me 39 minutes behind the 30-hour time, but I had probably lost what I gained with my long aid station break.

I had another five miles to the Last Chance aid station. It was mostly runnable, but my legs were feeling so tired and heavy that I decided to take it easy on this section. I had about 1:25 to go five miles. While I didn't want to go too easy, I knew that my legs could use a bit more walking as I would get into some of the toughest climbing of the course next.

I was walking really strong as I made my way through the trees. The course was beautiful at this point. The trees stood so tall and shaded the single track trail as I made my way along the mountain. With each step, I began to notice some pain in the front of my shins.

*What is that?* I thought. It almost felt like shin splints, but it was down lower towards my ankles. I started to move at a slow jog, which relieved some of the pain I was feeling. I remembered this happening at Javelina Jundred when I started walking more of the race towards the end.

*It's too soon for sore shins, Laura,* I thought to myself. *Don't do that again.*

As I trotted along, a few of the runners in our previous group caught up with me. We kept running along and another guy, Stuart, caught up to us too.

We continued to motivate each other as we came into the Last Chance aid station around 5:15 p.m. The cutoff for Last Chance was 5:30 p.m.

When we came in, we were each greeted by one volunteer who stayed with us the whole time we were in the aid station. I loved this because I didn't have to worry about finding someone to help me with anything. I handed the volunteer my bottles, asked him to add my Skratch powder, ice and water, and headed to the bathroom again.

I took a moment to try and collect my thoughts.

*Gosh I'm tired and my legs feel awful,* was the first thought to cross my mind. *This is so hard. I feel like crying. I feel like crap. I wish I could take a nap. Why did I decide to do this?*

I was in such a daze I just kept going through the motions of moving forward, but everything had become so hard.

When I came out of the porta-potty the volunteer helping me was standing there with both of my bottles ready.

*That's nice,* I thought to myself. *I didn't even have to go look for him.*

I glanced at him and said, "I feel like crap."

"Do you need to sit down?" he asked.

"No, I'll avoid the chair, I just feel crappy," I said.

Everything felt bad. My stomach wasn't upset, it just felt off. My feet hurt. I could tell I didn't have any blisters, but they were sore. My legs were tired. So tired. And my brain was starting to feel foggy. I was only 43 miles in and had a long way to go.

The volunteer put his hand on my back and guided me towards the food table to grab a snack. I picked up some Fritos and Oreos and we walked towards the exit of the aid station. There were more volunteers waiting there with ice and sponges to cool us down.

"Can you dunk my hat? And put some water on my arm sleeves?" I asked. The ladies running the cool down station were more than happy to help. They squeezed water all over my arms with giant sponges and one of them grabbed my hat and dunked it in ice water. I stuffed the Fritos in my mouth and tucked the Oreos in the pocket of my pack for later.

"I need ice in my sports bra, do you have just ice with no water?" I asked.

"Sure thing!" The ladies dumped a pitcher full of ice inside my bra. I was so tired I barely jumped when they poured the ice in. I was used to the chill and sting of the ice by now. Plus, I knew it would help get me up part of the climb to Devil's Thumb.

"Need anything else?" they asked.

"I think I'm good," I replied. "It's hot out here!"

"It is, and humid too! Keep drinking your fluids," they said. "You sure you don't want us to pour ice water over you?"

"No thanks," I said. "I don't want to start chafing."

They laughed in response, "We wouldn't want that either!"

My volunteer handed me my bottles and said, "You're doing great. Just keep moving forward. You are 4.5 miles from the Devil's Thumb aid station."

I walked out of the Last Chance alone, feeling crappy and knowing I had the most strenuous climb of the race directly in front of me.

# EIGHT
November 15, 2014

"Check out this picture," I texted Kelly one morning. I had attached the photo of a guy from Match.com running in what looked like a triathlon kit. He had liked the profile photo of me with my Javelina Jundred belt buckle so I decided to check him out.

"Isn't he cute?" I sent in another text.

"Oh! Is he a triathlete?" she texted back.

"He is! I'm going to send him an email."

I had been on Match.com for a few months and had dated around some, but hadn't met anyone that made me super excited. I was getting tired of the dating scene and decided to let my membership expire in December. I figured I'd message this guy and see what his story was before my membership was up.

I sent a short but sweet message, thanking him for liking my photo and asking him the usual first email questions. What was his name, where did he grow up, what did he do for fun, etc. I also asked what types of endurance events he participated in. I sent the email and waited eagerly for a reply. When I didn't hear from him for several days, and saw that he hadn't read my message, I figured maybe he just wasn't interested in me so I wrote him off. I had done enough online dating to know that you couldn't force anyone to like you. You just had to put yourself out there and hope for the best.

On November 30, I got a notification in the Match.com app. I opened it and it said I had a message from him. WHAT? I had written this guy off. What had taken so long? I opened his message and began reading.

*Dear Rnnrgrl3,*
*Thank you for the email! It looks like we have a lot in common. I had to like your photo. My dad and I are big fans of the Western States 100 and when I saw your Javelina buckle I figured you were big into ultras. Have you heard of Western States?*
*Joe*

I soon learned his name – Joe Chancellor – and that he grew up in Foresthill, but moved to Roseville when he was in elementary school. He was a triathlete and had just finished training for Ironman Tahoe (which ended up getting cancelled). He had done a 50K ultramarathon before and wanted to do another someday.

The conversations flowed from there. I told him all about getting into Western States and that I was still recovering from running Javelina Jundred four weeks prior. We discussed family and friends. We talked about religion and if we wanted to have children.

By the next day we had sent several emails back and forth and decided to exchange phone numbers so we could text or call. As a longtime Match.com user by that point in my life, I had made it a point to meet up with people I was interested in sooner rather than later. I found that the longer you waited, the more of a persona you built in your mind for the person, which often left you feeling led astray when they didn't turn out to be exactly like you envisioned.

We continued texting each other that week and got to know each other pretty well. Joe had recently moved to El Dorado Hills from Lincoln because his job was there, and he wanted to be closer to work.

That weekend we were both working at the California International Marathon. I was working at the race expo and aid station for Fleet Feet Sacramento, while Joe was volunteering at an aid station early in the morning. We decided that we should get together that Saturday evening for coffee after I finished work at the race expo.

On Friday I had tickets to go to a Kings game that evening with my friend Chris. He had a family emergency come up and ended up giving me the two tickets to the game. I texted Joe to see if he wanted to do a last-minute, first date to the Kings game. He was on board, so we made plans to meet at the Safeway near Arco Arena around 6:30 p.m. I offered to drive us over. This also allowed me to be able to leave early if he was a creep – a girl's gotta protect herself! – and he could walk back to his car about a half mile away at Safeway. Then we only had to pay to park one car too.

I jetted out of the race expo as quickly as I could that evening and ran home to change my clothes. I was in work gear and didn't want him to see me in that for our first date. I chose a slimming pair of dark jeans and a black long sleeve top. I had worn my hair down that day, thank goodness, so I fluffed it up and after grabbing a quick snack, took off to meet him at Safeway.

I'm always an early bird for "appointments." I hate to be late. I hate for people to be waiting for me. I was always early to class in college too. I just don't like to be late. So I arrived in the Safeway parking lot about 10 minutes early. I texted him right away to tell him I was there and what type of car I was in. He wrote back right away and told me he was almost there.

When he arrived he texted, "I'm here. I'm in a brick red FJ Cruiser."

"What's an FJ Cruiser?" I wrote back with a laughing emoji. I had no idea what kind of car that was.

He responded, "It's kind of like a Jeep but it's a Toyota. Where are you parked? I'll walk to you."

I told him and waited. I glanced out my passenger window and saw a tall, slender man with an athletic build striding confidently across the parking lot towards my car. *Is that him?* I thought to myself as this handsome man carrying a jacket in his hand made his way towards my car. *Oh my gosh! It is!* I checked myself in the mirror quickly and hopped out of my car walking around the back of it towards him.

"Joe?" I asked.

"Hey!" he said. I made my way towards him and gave him a hug.

"It's great to see you in person! You look just like your photos."

"Did you think I wouldn't?" he said inquisitively.

"Well, I've been on dates with a few guys who didn't look anything like their photos," I said with a laugh.

"That's awful!" he laughed.

We climbed into my car and headed towards Arco Arena, making small talk the whole way. Joe graciously paid for parking and we found a spot close to the entrance. Once we found our seats, Joe asked if I was hungry and offered to get me something. I said no as I had eaten quickly at home, and I had those pesky first date jitters that didn't leave me hungry at all.

We talked a lot throughout the game, discussing sports, running, triathlons, goals and what we were looking for from our lives. We didn't go too in depth with our backstories as the game was loud and we were surrounded by strangers, but that alleviated a lot of the stress from the date.

Joe spent the whole game leaning against the armrest, touching my arm. At one point he leaned forward with his elbows on his knees. He slowly glanced back at me, smiled and said, "I'm having such an awesome time with you."

I slowly smiled and said, "Me too." I'm sure I was blushing like a teenager!

When the game ended, we made our way out onto the concourse to leave the stadium. It was jam-packed, so Joe reached back and took my hand as we made our way among the throngs of fans trying to find the parking lot.

We chatted more on our way to the car and in the line of cars exiting the parking lot.

"I had such a great time with you," I said as I parked next to his FJ Cruiser.

"I had a great time too," Joe replied with a grin. "So, we had planned on our first date being coffee tomorrow. Would you still like to get coffee with me?"

"I'd love to!" I said. "I won't be done with work until around 6:30 after we clean up at the race expo."

"That works for me," he said. "How about I just pick you up at Fleet Feet?"

"That would be great," I replied.

We gave each other an awkward in car hug and he got out. *That may have been my last first date,* I thought to myself, giddy with excitement.

♦ ♦ ♦

The next evening, my team cleaned up at the race expo and moved everything back to Fleet Feet in record time, leaving me with enough time to get cleaned up at work before Joe would arrive at the store.

I stood nervously at the cash wrap in the front of the store talking to my co-workers. One of them asked, "Is he coming to get you?"

"Yeah, he will pull up out front I'm sure," I said.

Just then, he pulled up in his truck. "Oh my gosh. That's him!"

Several of the ladies I worked with came to the cash wrap. "Oooh, he's cute!" "He's so tall!" "Did you say he's a triathlete?" they said like a flock of hens.

"Stop it guys! He's going to hear you," I said, swatting them back.

He walked through the door and I walked up to give him a hug. "Hey," I said, blushing again.

"Hi," Joe replied, with a big smile. "You ready?"

"Yup. Let's go!" I said as he opened the front door, ushering me out into the night. I imagine my friends started giggling the minute the door closed.

Joe walked me to the passenger side of his car, opening the door for me and closing it once I was nestled inside. *He opens the door,* I thought to myself. *Bonus points!*

We drove several blocks away to Temple Coffee, and he took my hand as we crossed the street to go inside. The butterflies were rampant in my belly at the touch of his hand. We sat down with coffee the baristas had adorned with foam hearts. I'm sure they could tell it was a "first" date.

We discussed a lot of things in that second date. Our families and how we grew up. We talked about what we did as kids and where we went to school. We dove deeper into our running and triathlon backgrounds and talked about what we wanted in the future. We discussed our previous relationships, marriage and children and who we wanted to be as parents.

The conversation flowed so smoothly, soon it was nearing 11 p.m. and the baristas were cleaning up. We took them our cups and made our way out of the coffee shop back to his car. Joe politely opened the door and helped me into the car before making his way to the driver seat.

When we arrived back at Fleet Feet, I told him to pull around the back of the building to where my car was parked. He pulled into the gravel parking lot and we both got out of the car.

"I had such a great time," I said to him.

"Me too," he replied. "I'd love to see you tomorrow if you have time?"

"I'd really like that," I said, and we agreed to meet up for lunch after we each finished our duties at the marathon the next day.

We stood awkwardly for a moment, then Joe said, "I haven't done this in a long time so I'll just ask. Would it be OK if I kissed you?"

"That is so sweet," I responded. "Of course." And Joe took my face in his hands and gave me my last, first kiss. It was perfect. And I knew then, that this was the man I wanted to marry.

◆ ◆ ◆

Our next date was amazing, just like the previous two. We continued to get to know each other better and planned to get together again later that week.

The next day when I was at work, I was called down to the cash wrap to pick up a delivery. When I got downstairs, there was a vase with 18 red roses in it waiting for me.

"Oh my gosh!" I exclaimed. "Are those for me?"

"Apparently! Who sent them?" my coworker asked.

"I'm assuming Joe. Oh my gosh," I said again as I carried the heavy vase back to my desk.

When we were on one of our dates, Joe and I had talked about things from our childhood. I had told him the story of my 18th birthday when my Dad showed up in zero period band class with a vase of 18 red roses for me. He made me feel like the most special girl ever when he did that. And now Joe had done the same.

A few weeks later, Joe made the trip up to my hometown to meet my parents. Things were moving quickly, but nothing about it felt wrong. In fact, everything felt so right. Meeting my parents couldn't have gone any better. They loved him right away. My Mom and Dad could tell that there was something special about him. After they met Joe, I asked them if I could bring him to Kona, Hawaii with us for my birthday in January and they agreed.

On New Year's Eve that year, our family friends Karly and Johnny got married and my whole family was invited. Their wedding was at a church in Merced with the reception at a beautiful hall nearby. At one point during the reception, Joe and I were talking with my Mom about religion.

Mid-conversation Joe looked at me, smiled and said, "I want to marry you in a church in a full Catholic church mass."

My mouth dropped open, and I responded slowly, "OK."

He hopped up and went to get a drink at the bar with my Dad and when I turned around with my mouth still open, my Mom was sitting there with her mouth open too.

"Did that just happen?" I asked her.

"I heard it," Mom said with a smile.

"Oh my gosh!"

We came home from the wedding on New Year's Day, and on that Sunday, I took Joe to his first Catholic mass at a church close to his apartment. The church was Holy Trinity Parish in El Dorado Hills. It was a beautiful parish located on the top of a hill overlooking El Dorado Hills towards Sacramento. The location was perfect and just felt like the right place for Joe to begin his Catholic journey – and for me to reignite mine.

I hadn't been to Mass since Christmas – and before that, in months. I had drifted away from the Church and only went when I felt like I "should" (essentially when I was with my family). After we attended Mass, Joe said he was interested in learning more about becoming Catholic. He contacted the Church about the Rite of Christian Initiation for Adults (RCIA) classes they offered.

Soon after that Joe and I began attending Inquiry classes and learning more about the process. He met with the director of Faith

Formation and secured his spot in the upcoming session of RCIA to begin at the end of the summer. Joe's session would culminate with his baptism at Easter in March the following year. We were excited about the future, and continued attending church together there every Sunday.

Later that month we went to Kona, Hawaii with my parents and celebrated my 34th birthday. My family has been going to Kona for years, and we love it there. The slow-paced life and small town quality of Kona can't be beat. Plus, we usually stay at a condo complex within walking distance of some delicious restaurants and bars – and of course, right on the ocean. It's also on Alii Drive where the Ironman World Championship is held.

On our trip, we visited the Papakōlea Green Sand Beach, ran on Alii Drive every morning and enjoyed the sun, surf and sand. We spent my birthday zip lining in the forests in Hawaii and went to a delicious dinner with my parents. Joe and I were madly in love and I wanted to shout it from the rooftops!

When we came home and in February our relationship continued to evolve. Valentine's Day rolled around and we had even talked about really getting married someday. I couldn't believe the amazing life I had dreamt of was going to be a reality. And I had finally met the perfect man for me.

◆ ◆ ◆

Although we had fallen madly in love, I wasn't exactly the best version of myself. In the years prior, I had been in some pretty rough relationships. I had some tough times – as evidenced with my engagement ending – and while I felt my boyfriends treated me badly, I also wasn't the best partner. I was hard to deal with and an aggressive fighter, not physically, but verbally. I liked to yell. I had learned that when I was young and had been that way ever since. At the time, I believed it was just the way I was and everyone else had to deal with it. I wasn't as respectful as I should have been, because I wanted to control everything. I expected a lot and while I gave back in return, I didn't give what the other person needed in my relationships. I gave what I thought they needed and figured it was right.

In mid-February, Joe broke up with me, and rightfully so. I was rude and angry at times. I was controlling of everything because I wanted to know exactly what would happen or not in each situation. I suffered from strong anxiety that I didn't know how to deal with. I didn't know how to meet a partner where they were and give them what they needed in a relationship. While I loved him, I didn't treat Joe as well as I should have.

When Joe called to breakup with me, he said, "I get to choose what I put up with and I don't want this anymore." It drove a hole in my heart the size of the Grand Canyon. What was happening? Why was my so-called "perfect life" falling apart before my eyes?

That's when I knew I had to check myself. I finally saw what he saw. I saw that I didn't know how to love someone without being in control of our life together. I began to recognize that I had a lot of problems with admitting my fault in situations. I was awful at apologizing and angry when told I was wrong. I liked to yell and fight. I liked to feel like I was on top and winning each battle. And when I wasn't, or my anxiety or fear of abandonment took over, I was a mess. A dramatic mess of feelings that I couldn't deal with.

I can trace this back to growing up on the farm. My Dad is an amazing man and would give you the shirt off his back, but I now see that I took on his loud, argumentative style. Probably because I wanted him to love me and I wanted to be like him. I later realized that it wasn't the best way for me to be. I was a loving person but didn't know how to be loving without being angry too.

I told Joe that I was wrong and begged for forgiveness, but he stood firm. He told me that he didn't need that kind of attitude in his life. We could stay friends, but that's where he drew the line. I was beyond crushed. I found myself crying all the time and hiding behind my friend's desk at work when I just couldn't handle it.

I continued to be friends with Joe because I didn't want him out of my life. I also went to his RCIA classes with him as a supportive friend. We still talked a bit, but we were not dating.

My Western States coach told me that I had to apply this heartbreak and run mad. I couldn't let it drag me down and I had to work hard to overcome it. I needed to keep Western States in my view. This was easier said than done, and it worried me to no end. I simply didn't do well when my heart was broken. I had a tendency in the past to fall apart and lose all sense of life outside of my heartbreak. I couldn't let that happen when this race was on the line.

At the beginning of March, Joe was running the Way Too Cool 50K trail race. I was volunteering at the event to get in my service hours for Western States.

I saw him in his truck before the race and stopped to say hi.

"Hey! Good luck today," I said. "How are you feeling?"

"Thanks!" he replied with a smile. "I feel really good. We will see how it goes." I knew Joe would do great. He had been training extensively for it.

"Awesome! I'm working the finish line area so I'll try to see you when you come across."

I volunteered during the race and when Joe came through the finish line in a personal record time, I got to put his medal on him. We chatted for a bit after and he invited me to come by his house for dinner later that night. I agreed and headed over there after all my work at the race was done.

As we sat on his couch that night, there was a closeness and comfort in the space, and we broached the subject of our relationship.

"Listen," I said. "I don't want to get involved again unless this is going to be for real and we will work together to make it great. It takes two of us to put in the work. I'm ready to do all the work on myself but I know we both have to bring the best version of ourselves to the table."

"I know," he responded. "I know my past relationships haven't had the best communication and I will work on that too."

"So what does this mean?" I asked with a smile.

"Well, let's give this another try and see where it goes," he responded smiling. He sealed the agreement with a kiss and we agreed we would work on ourselves individually and as a couple.

After that, things were fantastic. While I wasn't perfect in my communication, I worked to make sure I wasn't being rude or controlling. It took a long time to help me straighten out, and I sought the expertise of a therapist during this time. Throughout this process, I discovered the right manner to talk to people. I also found the best ways to treat other people in my life. I realized things from growing up that had made me a fighter and adjusted my thoughts, so I didn't fall back into those attitudes and actions.

◆ ◆ ◆

As we grew closer in our relationship and talked more about marriage, we dove deeper into finances and where we both wanted to be in the future. While I didn't want to let Joe into my finances, mainly because I was ashamed of how bad things had gotten, I knew that I had to be vulnerable in the space so we could make things work for us. After my layoff, I had run up my credit cards because I could barely afford my home and I was spending above my means. We went through all my debt and we came up with a plan to help me get out of it.

As part of this, we realized that I would need to sell my condo because I could barely afford the payments with my current work and living situation. About a month after we got back together, Joe offered for me to move in with him so I could sell my condo and get out of debt.

The idea of moving my dog and me into a 900-square-foot, one-bedroom apartment with him didn't sound amazing. However, I knew I needed to do something drastic to get myself in the right place financially, so I took him up on the offer. Over the next month, I began selling most of my things so I could move into his apartment.

Around that time, I went on a trip to the Stagecoach Country Music Festival with my girlfriends. I know… I was in debt, but I had already paid for it before I met Joe so I decided to still go. While I was there, Joe texted me to let me know he had purchased my engagement ring. I was on Cloud 9! This was really happening!

I came home from my trip, finished selling my things and started moving everything into Joe's apartment. Although I had downsized quite a bit, while I was unpacking some things at Joe's apartment, it became clear that I hadn't downsized enough. So, I went about purging a second time. Over Memorial Weekend, we moved the last of my things to El Dorado Hills and put my condo up for sale. It sold within a month, with a cash offer and a quick escrow. We were on the road to a life together and I couldn't have been happier.

A month after we moved in together, we packed up all my running gear and headed to Squaw Valley for the Western States Endurance Run. We weren't engaged yet, but I knew that would be on the horizon after I ran the race.

Joe's love and support taught me how to be a better person. He not only taught me how to really love, but also taught me how to compromise, communicate, and fix the things I never wanted to admit needed fixing. Joe also taught me that God puts people in our life for a reason. He puts situations in our lives that may be difficult, but make us stronger and better for those around us.

Meeting Joe, breaking up with Joe and ultimately coming back together with him taught me to trust in the plan for my life. It taught me to believe there was a reason for everything I had been through. And even if it wasn't to be with Joe in the end, it was meant to be in my path. He expects the best from me, but also gives me the best of himself day in and day out. And he tells me whole-heartedly that he just wants me to be happy in life, whatever that may be. I hit the lottery when I found my Joe. I believe God put him in my path for a reason.

My relationship with Joe has taught me that tough things will always come your way. People will tell you things that you don't want to hear. But if you listen to them, you will find that what they have to say is actually really important and can help you be a better person.

You can't be stuck in your ways or you will stand in our own way to getting to something better. Having trust that there is someone or something out there for you is key! Staying positive and optimistic in the future is empowering because you never know whom God could put in your path.

# NINE

## Saturday, June 27, 2015 – Mile 43 - 5:22 p.m.

I walked away from the party at the Last Chance aid station in a bit of a daze. I knew I was going to have to work hard to get to Devil's Thumb within the cut-off time. I looked at my watch.

*I have 1:45 to do this section, but 2 miles of it is a straight up climb. Geez,* I thought.

I started to run at a trot along the fire road.

Then Stuart came up next to me. "Hey!" I said, "You made it!"

"Barely," he replied. "This is rough."

"It's OK. We've got this."

Stuart wasn't from California. I can't even remember where he was from, but I know the flat land state he lived in hadn't prepared him for how difficult this terrain was.

We continued down the fire road at a quick jog. We had about 2.5 miles to go until we reached Swinging Bridge at the bottom of the Devil's Thumb climb.

"We're going to have a long, single track downhill ahead until we reach Swinging Bridge. Then it's uphill for about a mile and a half to the Devil's Thumb aid station," I told Stuart between breaths. "It's a tough climb but I'm sure you can do it, you just have to push yourself and keep moving forward. Whatever you do, don't stop hiking up."

I could tell Stuart was struggling a bit and since we had been running together for a while, I felt that I should stick with him and help him out. We kept a fast pace until the gate that leads to the downhill to Swinging Bridge.

"You go ahead and lead," I said to him. "Just keep the pace quick."

Within the first few switchbacks along the trail I realized I should have led Stuart to the bottom. I was right on his heels the whole way down. I kept trying to hold back, but my body wanted to make up some time and blast down this hill. I tucked in behind Stuart and took the pace easy knowing I would need all the energy I had for the climb on the other side.

The heat was getting more intense as we made our way to the bottom. The air started to feel really heavy and wet. I'm sure part of that was from getting close to the river, but it also felt more humid outside the further we went.

As I moved along the trail behind Stuart, I went back and forth in my mind. I couldn't stop thinking about going faster.

*Do I pass him? Do I let him keep leading?* I looked at my watch. *We're losing minutes!*

Just as it started getting really frustrating for me, I saw Swinging Bridge through the trees. It was a glorious sight to behold. Just a few years before, the bridge had almost entirely burned in the American

Fire. The trail crews were able to rebuild it before the 2014 Western States race, and it was beautiful and stronger than ever.

"Look! There's Swinging Bridge!" I yelled to Stuart. "We're almost to the bottom!" As we reached the bridge, I checked my watch it read 13:03 hours for race time. That meant it was 6:03 p.m.

"We are cutting it really close Stuart," I said as we trotted across Swinging Bridge. "This climb takes me 55 minutes on my fastest day and the cutoff is 7 p.m. up there so we have to move. I'll take the lead you just stay on my heels, OK?"

"Sure," he responded, clearly quiet and out of breath.

I quickly pulled a caffeinated gel from my pack and downed it with some Skratch. I knew I would need the extra boost as I got part way up the mountain.

"Let's go Stuart. Hike like you mean it!" I yelled.

I started plowing my way up the mountain. Left, right, left, right. *Pump your arms, Laura. You know how to do this. You've practiced this so many times, now make it count!* I had run and hiked this part of the course four or five times in my training, so I knew that I could do it in 55 minutes if I focused and charged the mountain. I put my head down and did just that.

"How are you doing Stuart?" I yelled behind me, but heard nothing. I was on the third switchback of about 50 up the mountain. I looked over my shoulder and could see Stuart on the first switchback bent over with his hands on his knees.

"You OK Stuart?" I hollered at him.

He looked up and said yes, with weary eyes. We both knew this was the end of his day. But I was not about to let it be the end of mine. "Keep going Stuart, you got this!" I yelled as I tore up the hill.

I felt bad leaving Stuart behind. I knew that I couldn't help him though. I knew Stuart would eventually make it up to the top of the Devil's Thumb climb. It would be past the cutoff, but he would be OK.

In my experience trail running, I have always trained with groups of people and never ran these mountain trails by myself. On training runs it's known that you never leave a runner behind. Everyone who goes out together, returns together. But in supported races, unless someone is in distress, it's OK to leave them and focus on your race. You don't have to sacrifice your performance for someone else's race. Especially since things can go awry at any point for any runner. That is why there are safety patrol runners and horses bringing up the back of races like Western States.

*Worry about yourself Laura, get this done!* I was really pumping myself up now. I tried to keep a good uphill pace. The climb to Devil's Thumb is about one and a half miles up the side of the canyon. There are switchbacks the entire way to the top and the incline is unrelenting. You climb about 1,500 feet of elevation in the 1.5 miles from the river to the top. Keeping your pace going is critical as it's so hard to get started again when you stop.

As I ascended each of the switchbacks, I thought of all the training runs I had done with my training partners. So many runners had joined me on the journey to Western States: Dan, Jen, Linda, Pam, Brad, Bob, Mo, Dee, Joe and countless others. They had pushed me through this tough portion of the course so many times to help me be prepared for this exact moment.

I laughed out loud when I thought of my friend Linda telling me to turn on the "Granny Gear" when we would hike up to Devil's Thumb in training. The Granny Gear is the lowest gear on a bicycle, allowing you to ride up a hill with your feet moving fast, but your gear intensity low. I pictured myself turning on the Granny Gear just like her so I could move faster but efficiently up the mountain.

My glutes and quads were burning as I pushed through each step to move faster. *No pain, no gain Laura. You got this.* It was really hot now. The ice I had in my sports bra was almost all melted. About halfway to the top I came across the first runner sitting on the side of the trail. The runner was sitting with his head in his hands and elbows on his knees.

"You OK?" I asked as I came close to him.

"Yeah, just feeling done," he replied.

"You got this, follow me up the mountain! Let's go!" I said in an energetic voice. I was trying my best to pump him up, but I couldn't stop to help him either. Just like the climb up to Robinson, I told myself that if I ever came across someone in distress, passed out, unconscious or whatever, I would give up my race to help a fellow human. However, for runners who were sitting but still functional, I would only cheer them on – then worry about my race.

I came across about five more runners in the same situation. One of them even laid his head on a rock and told me he was going to just rest his eyes for a minute. Each were down and to the point of possibly giving up. I reminded them that each step forward was one step closer to the finish and further from a cutoff, but they probably didn't care to hear what I had to say.

I knew this part of the course so well and knew I was getting close to the top. I was coming up on the last set of switchbacks when I looked out to my left off the mountain. The views up there are beyond spectacular. It feels like you can see forever down the canyon.

As I took the right-hand turn onto the first of two long switchbacks to the top of the mountain, I could see Devil's Thumb rock directly in front of me. That's when I heard it: the single horn blast. I only had 10 minutes. I knew I would hear the horn, but when you actually hear the horn it brings a whole new sense of urgency to you.

I started hiking faster than I ever had before.

"Do not give up, Laura!" I told myself. "You have come too far to have this be the end. Get up this mountain!"

I saw a lady with a walkie-talkie at the end of the first switchback. *Just get to her,* I thought. *She's waiting for your bib number.* I power hiked directly towards her, focusing on pushing through my glutes but being light on my feet to keep my turnover quick.

I got to her and said, "Bib 1-2-6".

"I already called it in, you got this! Get up there!" she exclaimed.

I sped up the last of the two long switchbacks to the top, where I encountered volunteers everywhere.

"I have a drop bag," I said to the first volunteer I saw. Then a woman walked towards me holding my headlamp and Pepsi from my drop bag.

"1-2-6! I got you right here," she yelled to me. "Let's go, what do you need?"

"Um, I don't know," I said.

"Walk over here," she replied as she guided me towards the food and water table. "I'm going to tuck your headlamp in the back of your pack, OK?"

"Sure, that works. I'll take the Pepsi," I said taking the soda from her and putting it in my pack pocket.

I handed her my empty bottles and asked her to fill them with water and Skratch powder as I had done at the previous aid stations. She took off with them while another volunteer handed me some Coke.

"Do you want some fruit? How about pretzels?" another woman asked.

"That all sounds great," I replied. "I don't think I can eat it before I get out of here though."

"No worries honey, we're making you a to-go baggie right now," she said as she filled a baggie with strawberries, and another with pretzels.

"Here are your handhelds, let's go," the first volunteer said as she walked back to me. She walked me around the table and right out of the aid station. "Your next aid is at El Dorado Creek in 5 miles. You made this cutoff by six minutes, but you've got to keep moving to make the next one."

"Thank you so much! You are all amazing," I said as I walked away from the aid station.

*Wait,* I thought. *I made it with only 6 minutes to spare? Gosh that was close!*

I continued to walk along the top of the mountain carrying my baggies of fruit and pretzels. I looked down and adjusted my bottles in my other hand. *Holy geez,* I thought. *I barely made that cutoff. How am I still in this?*

This section of the trail is wider, with enough space for two runners to move along side by side. It's relatively flat or rolling across the top of the mountain past the pump. I knew I could run pretty much all of it, as well as the downhill to El Dorado Creek on the other side.

*You know this section… you can do this. Just get moving.* I told myself as I started at a trot. I had trained this section so many times it was like coming home. As I made my way along between the trees I let my mind wander and relax, not stressing about time or location. My mind needed a rest.

*Just run,* I told myself. *Enjoy the ease of this section.*

That's when I looked up and saw my first running coach, Ken, walking towards me. He was wearing his signature red hat and was beaming with the biggest smile.

"Ken!" I yelled. "I am so happy to see you!"

"Well, hello!" he yelled back. I was so excited to see someone I knew, hear their voice and be able to tell them how hard the race had been. I couldn't have been any more elated to be in his presence. Ken had driven up to what we refer to as the pump, parked and walked back on the trail to cheer for me and other runners. The pump is a hand pump up on the top of the mountain that we would use often to refill our hydration packs and bottles on training runs. There is a dirt road that drives into this pump and the Devil's Thumb aid station from Foresthill Road. The Pump is about a mile past the Devil's Thumb aid station and is used as an aid station location for other races and training runs on the course.

"Congratulations! You just made the toughest cutoff of the whole race!" he said when I got to him. Ken had run Western States before; he had even attempted it two times before he finished it, so he knew all the ins and outs of the course.

"I did?" I asked

"Yes, based on the timing, this is the toughest cutoff to make when you're at the back of the pack."

"Wow. Well I'm so glad that's over!" I said. "Ken, it's been so hard. I can't even explain to you. This is awful."

"But you're doing it and you know the whole course from here. Just keep going. You've got this now, Laura." His confidence in me was just the boost I needed.

"Thank you, Ken," I replied with a smile.

"Now get moving and I'll see you in Foresthill." With that I took off at a trot down the trail and he turned around to wait for more runners to come through.

"Thank you so much for coming out, Ken! Seeing you was just what I needed!" I yelled back.

As I came up on the pump, I saw a few horse trailers in the parking area. At Western States, there are sweepers – also known as safety patrol runners. Towards the end of the race, there are horses with riders who sweep the course to make sure everyone makes it out safely.

As approached the area with the horses, their riders yelled out a friendly and encouraging, "Hello!"

"Hi there. I have to stay ahead of you, right?" I replied.

"Yup! But you look good. You should be fine. Have a good run!" they said.

"Thank you! Don't sweep me up!" I half-joked as I moved past them and down the trail.

*Note to self,* I thought. *Do not let the horses catch you. You are not getting swept up at this race!*

# TEN
## January 26, 1981

A few days after I was born, my parents brought me home to our 120-acre farm in Durham, California, where we raised 1,000 dairy cows. My Dad came to the United States from Holland when he was five years old. He arrived here with his mom, dad and sister and they started a life, eventually purchasing the dairy farm where my parents still live and work.

My Dad began working full-time on our family farm when he was 19 years old. He had attended Butte Community College for a semester before he decided to stop going, since his plan was to take over the farm anyway. My Mom and Dad met in the milking parlor at her family dairy farm in Willows, California. They dated and got married, and Mom moved across the valley to join Dad in taking over our family farm. When she was younger her parents told her NOT to marry a dairyman. So, she did. As did her sister, and their brother took over the Willows family farm. Another generation of dairy farmers had started.

Dairy life is a lot of work. I remember all the times Dad and Mom would have to get up in the middle of the night to deliver a baby calf. Or when equipment would break and Dad would send my Grandma somewhere to pick up a part or something he needed.

Life with animals never stops. You always have to take care of them. They always have to be milked, fed, vaccinated, provided for when they are sick and cleaned up after. You have to put a roof over their heads, make sure they are in a safe pasture and love on them as well. It's a lot like having a child. Except there are 1,000 of them and they don't talk back to you!

My earliest memories of our dairy are following Dad around as he walked through the farm doing his chores. One day in particular, I remember we were walking past the generator building and I was trying to keep up with him.

"Dad, I have to skip to keep up with you!" I laughed as I quickly skipped alongside him.

"Well, keep up," he replied. I did, as fast as I could so I could hang out with my Dad.

Another time, back when I had a tricycle, I had ridden it so much and so hard that the plastic pedals had broken off and all that was left was the metal arm sticking out. The metal arms hurt my feet when I would ride around barefoot, so one day I pushed my tricycle out to the shop where our farm employee Israel was working.

I barged in with my trike, put my hands on my hips and said, "Are you gonna fix my bike or what?!"

Israel laughed as he asked what I needed, and I proceeded to tell him I had broken the pedals off and needed new ones. He went to work on it and welded some fabulous metal pedals on that are still there to this day.

Growing up we were taught that there was nothing we couldn't do or accomplish. We were creative and inventive all the time. Many times, I could be found in the shop building something with a hammer, nails and some scrap wood I found. Or I was inventing some new project I would need Dad to help me with later since I wasn't allowed to use a saw. We built forts and rock houses in the back of the barns. We played in the cotton seed piles until the dusk-to-dawn lights came on.

There were many tough times working on the farm. We saw animals die daily. We were no stranger to baby calves being stillborn. We also saw cows get sick and have to be put down. We saw the milk prices go up and then plummet. We knew that we wouldn't be going on big family vacations because there were always animals to care for, but when we did get a family vacation, we savored every moment of it.

I remember one time was especially hard for all of us, especially my Dad. We were out in the barn with a cow that was in labor. After a while of being in labor, my Dad checked the cow and found out that the baby wasn't going to be able to deliver naturally because it was breeched and had gotten one leg stuck during labor.

"Linda, call the vet. We need to take her in," he said as he wiped sweat from his head.

"You think?" she replied.

"Yeah, the baby is breech and one leg isn't coming. I don't know if the vet will be able to get it out or if we will need to do a cesarean section but I can't do anymore here," he said matter of factly.

The next thing I knew Dad and a few farm employees had used the tractor to scoop up the cow and gently roll her into our cattle trailer.

"Dad, can I come with you?" I asked. I had always been curious about births on the farm and everything my Dad did with the animals.

"Sure, get in the truck," he replied.

We drove the 30 minutes to Orland to take the cow to the vet. Dad seemed confident that the vet would be able to help this cow deliver a healthy calf. We arrived and the vet and his assistants carefully unloaded the cow into the exam area.

After checking the cow, the vet let us know the verdict. "Looks like this baby is definitely turned around. Let's do the cesarean and see how it goes," he said.

After the procedure was over, the vet came out to give us an update. "It isn't good news," he said. "We lost the baby and the mom."

"Shit," my Dad said as he dropped his head.

"There was nothing you could do, Leo," the vet said gently. "You did everything you could."

My Dad has always been an animal lover. He was always great with the cows and while each one is a way to make money from milk production, more than that, each one is a living being. It's never easy to lose a cow. Especially when you've worked so hard to help the cow and the baby survive.

Dad and I got back in the truck for the 30-minute drive home. As we were leaving town, he pulled into the gas station and parked. "I'll be right back," he told me. After a few minutes he walked out with two sodas and a bag of chips in his hand.

"Here you go," he said as he climbed in and handed me a Crème Soda, my favorite road trip drink. I smiled back at him as he opened his Dr. Pepper and tossed me the bag of chips. "Open those up," he instructed. I did as I was told and he pulled out on the highway heading home. We sat in silence on that drive, enjoying our sodas and chips. We didn't have to talk. I already knew my Dad didn't want to discuss the situation as he had done everything he could to help that cow. And I knew that everything would be OK, even though the experience had been hard on him. Things on the farm always worked out in the end, no matter how hard they were.

There were many wonderful times too. Our family ate breakfast and dinner together every day. We were so lucky that we got to share stories from our day, hear our parents talk about the farm and learn about the business. There was nothing we wouldn't discuss with our parents. We talked about being bullied in school, getting good grades on tests or issues with friends. We talked about sports as we all read the morning paper. And my family humored me as I discussed the newest music craze or my love of the New Kids on the Block, and later, The Backstreet Boys.

My brother and I were both members of our local 4-H club from age seven through high school. We raised dairy cows and participated in community projects like picking up walnuts and singing carols at Christmas. My brother took wood working and I chose sewing. We were officers and then junior leaders in our 4-H groups. 4-H taught us so much about hard work and dedication. It taught us to challenge ourselves. We learned that if we didn't put our full effort into whatever we were doing, we wouldn't perform well. My brother had an amazing cow, Bertha, that won Grand Champion two years in a row at the Silver Dollar Fair. I wasn't as lucky with my cow, Margaret, but it was still fun to show. I was much better at sewing and won the Butte County 4-H Fashion Review my junior year of high school when I made a formal dress from the movie Titanic.

When I was in eighth grade, my Dad sat my brother and I down for a serious chat. Dad said that he didn't want us to take over the farm unless we were 100% sure we wanted that life. He didn't want us to feel obligated to keep the family business alive just because we "should." Honestly, neither of us wanted to take it over. We knew how hard the farm life was just by watching our parents' everyday. They were born to take care of the animals. It was in their blood. While my brother Leigh and I enjoyed it, we didn't have the passion for it like they did. We wanted to start our own adventures and live our own stories. My brother wanted to become a physical therapist and I wanted to do something outside of the small town we lived in, though I wasn't sure what that was yet.

We were raised to work hard and recognized that nothing came for free. Our parents expected us to get good grades and do our homework. They also provided consequences when we didn't do the right thing. I know I was grounded a lot more than my brother for breaking the rules, but I was more of a rebel than he was. I was the one always out running around with friends while my brother was home studying.

We had chores to do around the farm and the house. We mowed the lawns on the weekends and helped feed the calves. We cleaned the house and set the table. We washed the cars and trucks and emptied the dishwasher. We helped make dinner and do the grocery shopping. We did anything they asked us to do, though we could be caught whining about it, because it was just the way farm life worked.

Growing up on a farm taught me that the sun never sets on a family business. When you own a small business, there's always something to do. There is always a bill to pay and always tomorrow to think about. There are employees to hire and fire, and products to sell. Hard work will pay off, but it will always be hard work no matter how you slice it. And every day no matter what, you have to get up and keep going. You can't call in sick. You can't do the project tomorrow. You have to do it today and keep moving forward, because tomorrow there will be another project to complete.

I also learned that it could be the most rewarding job on the planet. My parents have worked side-by-side for more than 40 years. They have seen our farm go from a dairy, to a heifer-raising operation, to now a beef cattle business and walnut orchards. My parents are in their 60s now and have toned their work back a bit, but the job still drives them to get up every single day. They love their life on the farm. They love that most of their grandkids live in a house right next door. They love that they get to see the fruits of their labor every single day.

How is this like running 100 miles? How much quit do you have in your system? When something seems hard, do you throw in the towel? When you run 100 miles you don't have a choice but to keep going to the end. The race will get hard. Really, really hard. You'll hit spots when you want to quit. You'll hit spots where things are great. But in the end, you have to put in the work and finish. While there aren't any animals that will die in the 100-mile process, you have to live with your decision to quit an ultra. You have to live with knowing you could have kept going if you pushed yourself a little harder.

Growing up on a farm wasn't easy. It was hard. But determination will take you far in the life of a farmer. My childhood was hard. It was rough and unrelenting, much like running 100 miles. I never thought 100 miles would be easy, because life is never easy.

And going through the tough parts of farm life allowed me to push through 100 miles better than I ever would have anticipated.

◆ ◆ ◆

Mentally, when you run 100 miles, you have to be ready to run for a long time. You have to get very comfortable with being uncomfortable. And you have to rely on yourself to stick it out and get the job done. You can't just give up. Just like you can't give up on the farm animals. Who will take care of them if you don't? Who will run the 100 miles if you don't? (That's right, no one.)

So, the next time that you think you can't do something or you want to call it a day when you shouldn't, remember that sometimes you just have to push through the hard stuff because it's what you do. And because it's the only way you will get to the finish line. On your own two feet.

# ELEVEN
## Saturday, June 27, 2015 – Mile 49 - 7:10 p.m.

As I jogged along down the dirt road, I carefully ate the strawberries the Devil's Thumb volunteers had packaged for me. They were the most delicious strawberries I had ever eaten, probably because I was starting to feel hungry from the climb up Devil's Thumb. I tucked away the trash and stowed the baggie of pretzels in my pack as well. I adjusted my handheld bottles onto both hands.

The trail cuts to the left into a single-track that parallels the fire road towards Deadwood Cemetery. The trail was covered in pine needles from the towering trees overhead and scattered with downed trees, shrubs and grass. It's honestly one of the most beautiful parts of the trail. It's easy to run as the ground seems softer than other areas, but not like sand. The entire scene is peaceful and welcoming.

Maybe it was because I had run it so many times, or maybe it was because I knew I would see my crew in a few miles, but something in me finally felt amazing at this point of the race. As I cruised along, I just felt good. Light on my feet. Hydrated. Happy. Optimistic for the first time in many miles.

I continued running the gradual uphill and then the declines towards Deadwood Cemetery. The trail merged back in with the dirt road for about 100 yards with the entrance to Deadwood Cemetery directly in front of me. I took the left-hand trail down the hill beginning my descent towards El Dorado Creek.

When I would train this part of the course I would either start in Foresthill or Michigan Bluff and do an out and back through this section. My coach and I had a goal for me to know exactly how long it would take me to get from one point to the next on every section of the course I could train. In my training I had consistently run the section from Devil's Thumb to the bottom of El Dorado Creek in 1:15.

*I left Devil's Thumb around 6:58 p.m. so I should be able to get there by about 8:15 p.m.* I thought. However, I knew that when I left Devil's Thumb, I was still 49 minutes behind the 30-hour time.

*I need to figure out how to make up some more time.*

The trail is about a three-mile downhill trek into the bottom of the canyon where you reach El Dorado Creek. This section of the course is easy to run, and one of my favorites to charge down because it's so fast. There are several switchbacks that can cut down on your speed but it's a very forgiving part of the trail with a smooth dirt path and not too many rocks or roots to hop over compared to earlier sections of the race. This is a section you can run too hard and burn out your quads, so you have to be careful. I had practiced hiking up and running down this section of the course so many times in my training that it felt like coming home.

*This is where I can make up time. Turn it on, Laura.*

I pranced my way down the hill knowing every twist and turn of the trail by heart. Through the dry parts up top, down through the areas covered with walls of ivy and poison oak, and then surrounded by manzanita bushes. Along the switchbacks where you start to hear the roar of the creek, and across the limestone rocks littering the sharp corners. My quads felt great and I stayed light on my feet to keep my turnover fast.

As I approached the last few sections, I started to get really excited because I knew there was a great aid station across the bridge. On the final switchbacks, when I heard the roar of the creek, I also started to hear the hum of the aid station. I came down the final descent, took the bridge quickly and walked down the other side towards the aid station.

"Welcome to El Dorado Creek!" one volunteer said. "What can we get you?" I handed them one bottle to fill with water and Skratch powder then grabbed a few chips.

The first thing I noticed when I got down to the aid station was that the sun was already behind the mountain. While it was summer time and still hot outside, there was a chill that came over my shoulders.

*Is that dehydration?* I thought as picked up a cup of water, downing it in a few swigs. "Can I have some more please?" I asked and a volunteer refilled my cup from a pitcher.

*I need to stay hydrated for this part,* I thought. *The sun may be going down, but it's still hot out here.*

"Do you have soup?" I asked.

"Sure thing!"

A volunteer handed me a warm cup of soup. It definitely sounds counter productive to have warm soup on a hot day, but it sure was delicious. The salt and broth tasted so amazing as I sipped it. Then I began to realize just how sore my shins were from all the walking I had done earlier.

*Not again!* I thought.

"Do you have any Tylenol?" I asked the aid station as my shins continued to burn.

"Yes, right here," they replied. I took two and drank them down with the soup. I knew that taking NSAIDS or Ibuprofen was a no-no because it could cause kidney issues, but I figured at least some Tylenol would take the edge off the pain in my legs.

"You doing OK?" they asked.

"Sure. Just sore," I replied.

"Understandable. Don't stand around here too long. When you finish that soup, we are kicking you out."

"Thank you," I laughed. I knew I was going to need them to move me on my way. "Can one of you grab my headlamp from the back of my pack for me?" The volunteer came around the table, retrieved my headlamp and handed it to me.

"What time is it?" I asked as I secured the lamp on top of my hat.

"You came in at 8:22," the aid station timer replied. "And the cutoff at Michigan Bluff is 9:45 p.m. That gives you about 1:20 to get up to Michigan Bluff."

I quickly thought back to my training. I had always hiked out of El Dorado Creek in about 1:10. *I need to move.*

I downed the rest of my soup, grabbed my bottle, thanked the volunteers and walked out of the aid station towards the first part of the climb.

"You've got this," I told myself as I straightened my headlamp. "You've done this climb so many times. One foot in front of the other, march up this hill and get there in time."

I quickly ate another caffeinated gel, tucking the trash in my pack. I started hiking fast – the fastest I possibly could. I passed a few runners who were taking their time up the first part. The climb from El Dorado Creek to Michigan Bluff was almost three miles, uphill the whole way. You could run a few parts of it, but I could hike faster than I could run so I pumped my arms and moved as fast as I could.

The shadows were gone, and the light was dimming a lot faster than I thought it would so I turned on my headlamp for a little extra light. That's when I realized the light on my headlamp was a little more faint than I remembered it being.

*Hmm, I wonder if the batteries are low?* I thought. But I kept moving. I powered along, up the switchbacks, along the side of the mountain, through the areas covered in quartz rock and across the a few small water crossings. My light was getting dimmer and dimmer the longer I hiked.

*Don't let it slow you down. You can still move forward. You can see. It's not that dark yet.*

I crossed the only real creek crossing on this section and made my way to the last three long uphill parts of the climb. That's when I started to realize that I could barely see. My light was so dim and there was no twilight left. I tripped over roots and rocks with each step.

*I'm not going to make it,* I thought. *There's no way!*

I had caught up to a few runners and started following their lights just so I knew the general direction of the trail.

Then I saw two lights coming towards me. It looked like a headlamp and a waist lamp on one person. Just then I tripped and fell to my knees, landing on my bottles with my hands.

"Shit!" I yelled.

"Fancy seeing you here!" I heard Brad's voice say.

"Brad!" I exclaimed. "You're here! Are you supposed to be here?"

"Yeah, they let pacers come down to get you when we get close to the cutoff," Brad replied. "Let's get out of here. Follow me."

"I can't see a thing," I replied. "Thank goodness you found me. Your lights are a life saver."

"Follow my lights and move. We don't have a lot of time."

"Am I going to make it, Brad?" I asked in a shaky, scared voice.

"Yes, you're going to make it but you have to move," he replied sternly.

We started charging up the hill through the last two long uphill sections until we reached the road in Michigan Bluff.

I yelled out my bib number to the volunteer checking us in as we ran past. We trotted down the gravel road into Michigan Bluff, past dimly lit houses and into the rowdy aid station. As I came up on the right-hand turn to go into the aid station, Joe and Andy were standing there waiting for me.

"Hi guys!" I exclaimed. "Brad came and found me!"

"He did!" they responded. "You look great!"

I turned the corner to go behind the ropes into the aid station.

"I feel good!" I yelled at them. "My headlamp almost died out there so I could barely see when Brad found me. He's a lifesaver."

I called out my number again as I neared the aid station tents.

"1-2-6 in!" I yelled and walked under the tent to the hydration and food area. The volunteers quickly took my empty water bottle and filled it for me, adding the Skratch powder as well.

"Laura, we're right over here set up in the street," Joe yelled to me as I moved past the hydration table to the food table.

"Can I get some soup please?" I asked.

"Sure! Do you want rice or no rice?" a volunteer responded.

"Rice please," I said.

"We have quesadillas too. Do you want one?" another volunteer offered.

"Yes!" I said excitedly.

They handed me a steaming cup of soup and a plate with a quesadilla on it.

"Can I have some of those pretzels too?" I asked.

A volunteer grabbed a bowl and tossed in a handful of pretzels then asked, "Anything else?"

"I think I'm good," I replied as she set the bowl on top of the quesadilla. "Thank you all!" I yelled as I turned and made my way toward the other end of the aid station.

"Oh wait, my bottles!" I yelled. The volunteer filling them ran over to me and tucked them under my arm as I headed out of the aid station area.

My crew was right there waiting for me as I exited onto the street. "Where are we set up?" I asked.

"Right here!" Carol yelled as I walked towards her to the blanket they laid out in the street.

"What's on my list?" I asked her when I got close.

"We will get everything you need," Carol replied. "Go ahead and eat your food and we will take care of everything else."

In a flurry of movement my crew began to add and remove things I needed for the next section of the course. Someone took my plate and cup, holding them in front of me so I could use my hands. My crew pulled off my dead headlamp and my hat with the neck cooling panel and handed me a fresh, dry hat.

"Put this on backwards," Carol instructed and I did as she said.

"I'm so excited to see you all!" I said to her, wide-eyed and probably looking a little crazy. "What time did I come in?" I asked.

"9:30, 15 minutes before the cutoff."

"Here's your big headlamp," Carol said, handing the "train light" headlamp I had borrowed from Ken for the nighttime portion of the race. The headlamp made a ray of light that lit up a huge area in front of me so I would have nothing to worry about when looking for the trail. It also had a large battery pack on the back so I wouldn't have to replace the batteries at all.

I put the headlamp on over my hat, between taking sips of soup and bites of my quesadilla.

Carol unhooked my watch from my wrist, then simultaneously stopped my watch and started my second watch I had borrowed from my co-worker, Justin, the same guy who had sold me my first pair of running shoes. "Here, put this on." She instructed.

I put the watch on carefully. "What was my time on the last watch?" I asked so I could keep that in mind moving forward.

"16:35," Carol said as she held out a knuckle light to me. "OK. You're good to go. Get out of here."

"Let's go Laura," Brad said. "I've got your pretzels. Leave the plate and carry the quesadilla and soup cup. I'll take the trash when you're done."

I handed the plate to Carol in exchange for the quesadilla and knuckle light. Joe handed me my full bottles with refilled Skratch powder pouches and kissed me goodbye. I tucked the bottles under my arm as I ate the quesadilla.

"Thank you guys!" I yelled with my mouth full as Brad and I walked up the street out of Michigan Bluff.

"Holy heck, that was crazy!" I said to him.

"Yes, you have quite the pit crew." My crew was a well-oiled machine and I knew it.

"How many minutes do we have before the cutoff?" I asked. We were already clear from it, but I wanted to know how close we were.

"We're about 10 minutes ahead of it. Let's move so we can make up more time," Brad said.

"What time is it?" I asked.

He looked at his watch. "9:38," he replied.

I had made up a few minutes on the 30-hour time with my climb from El Dorado Creek. The actual climb had taken me 1:08, which was less than my training run times had been. But I was still behind the 30-hour mark by 40 minutes. The 30-hour mark got a bit more forgiving from this point of the race on, based on terrain changes and difficulty. Plus, you're able to pick up a pacer which can help keep paces steady since you have someone with you to not only push you, but to think for you as you are running.

Brad was my pacer. He and I had met while I was working at Fleet Feet Sacramento. He was an avid trail runner and a really friendly, entertaining guy. I knew he would be a good fit as a pacer for me, so I asked him to join me when I found out I got my Western States spot. He had also paced me for the last 15 miles of the Overlook 50 Miler in preparation for Javelina Jundred the year before. Brad was great at keeping me moving and entertained, and he never got mad at me when I yelled at him in a sleep deprived, exhausted stupor.

"Here, eat some more pretzels," Brad said as he pushed the bowl of snacks in front of my face.

I took a few. "I'm good now, we can get rid of the rest." Brad folded the bowl up and tucked it with the pretzels in the pocket of his pack.

We hiked along Gorman Ranch Road for what seemed like eternity. There were a few downhill areas we ran, but mostly we were hiking uphill towards Foresthill. We made the right-hand turn on Chicken Hawk Road for the long climb leading to the rolling hills on top of the mountain. We were still on a dirt and gravel road, but soon that road would turn off onto another dirt fire road and then onto a single track down to Volcano Creek.

Brad moved in front of me. "Just follow my feet and let's move up this hill," he said. I followed his lead. That's the beauty of a pacer. They can help you keep your wits about you when things start to go south, or you want to slow down. I had made a deal with Brad and my other pacer Bob that I would just follow them and do whatever they wanted me to do so we could get to the finish.

"This has been insane, Brad," I said as we hiked. "I never imagined my day would go like this."

"You're telling me," he replied. "To be honest, Bob and I didn't know if you'd make to this far based on the times."

"You talked to Bob?" I asked.

"Yeah, we've been talking the whole time you've been running. We were really worried before you got to Robinson," he said quietly.

"Me too!" I replied with a giggle. "I didn't think I'd even make it there! But I kept telling myself that I had to leave everything out here so if I didn't make it, I knew I'd done everything I could."

"Oh, we know! You've definitely been beating the odds for the whole race," Brad said excitedly.

"Brad?" I asked. "Do you think I'm going to make it?"

"Yes," he replied. "But you have to push this whole time. We're not going to dilly-dally. Aid stations will be fast. While you're ahead of the cutoffs, you're still behind the 30-hour so we need to make up that time."

"OK. I'll do whatever it takes," I said confidently. "It will hurt way worse to not get a buckle than any pain you could put me through anyway." I laughed, but I knew that was the truth. Finishing this race is what I had trained for almost two years to do. I knew I wanted to run 100 miles, and I knew I wanted to finish Western States. I wasn't going to let anything stop me.

"What's Bob up to?" I asked.

"He's been stalking the website. We made a deal that I need to just get you to him around the 30-hour mark and he will do the rest," Brad said. "We will make up as much time as we can and then he will take it from there."

"Sounds like a plan."

We were nearing the top of the road where we make a left onto a rolling downhill and flat to the single track. I knew this section was very runnable after the times I had gone through it in my training. And once on the single track it was a quick downhill with switchbacks to the river crossing at Volcano Creek.

As we made the left-hand turn, Brad turned over his left shoulder to look at me and we both began to move at a trot. He didn't have to ask. I knew it was time to run. We cruised along the road with our headlamps illuminating the way.

One piece of advice Ken had given me was that most people move slower at night not only because they are tired, but also because they can't see as well. By using a very bright headlamp you allow yourself to really see and therefore run faster. With this in mind, I had chosen to carry one knuckle light to shine right in front of me as we ran. I could hold the light easily with my bottles, so I always had light in front of me, even if I turned my head. I wanted to leave nothing to chance on the course and with those and my train head lamp, it looked like daylight even in pitch black darkness.

We continued down the rolling hills to the flat area across the top of the mountain. There was less covering along the road so you could see the sky well. It was so quiet as we made a slight right onto the single track towards Volcano Creek. I was really glad I had the train lamp as we entered the wooded portion of the course. The tree cover had blacked out any ambient light from the moon and the lights made it feel less creepy.

Brad continued to run in front of me. He moved at a good clip but never too fast for me to keep up with him. He looked back often to make sure he wasn't losing me. We would chat some, but with the darkness it was easier to focus on the running and foot placement than it was to talk.

We made the descent to Volcano Creek, and towards the bottom started to hear the water rushing over the rocks. While it wasn't a large river crossing, it still required very careful steps to get across the water. This was definitely a crossing where your feet would get wet, much like Duncan Creek miles before.

As I made my way down to the creek, Brad went ahead and searched for a good spot to cross. He made his way across pointing out rocks for me to focus on. I followed him carefully, stepping on the slippery rocks under the water. It was about 10:30 p.m. and you would think the water would feel cold, but with how hot my feet had been all day, I welcomed the water over my shoes. It was actually refreshing and comfortable with how hot and humid it had been. All day part of me wanted to sit in the water for a minute, but I knew that wouldn't be a good idea at this point.

Brad began hiking out of the creek at a solid pace and I stayed right on his heels.

"It's not too far to the bottom of Bath Road," Brad said.

"Will my crew be there?" I asked.

"They said they will, but let's just focus on getting there."

We moved quickly uphill on the single track and switchbacks, making a right-hand turn onto the sandy, rocky terrain that took us to the bottom of the paved portion of Bath Road. As we came through the gate, we saw lights and heard voices up on the road pavement.

"Laura?" I heard Joe call out.

"I'm here!" I yelled back.

"Woohoo!!" Everyone started screaming. Not only were Joe and Andy there (Carol had stayed in Foresthill to set up everything for my crew stop), Scott from Sacfit met us too.

"Hi guys!" I said as I got closer. "Thanks for coming down!"

I was so excited to see people I knew. And knowing that they got to hike and run all the way into Foresthill with me really started to raise my spirits. At this point of the race, I was starting to get tired. Not just exhausted from the exercise all day, but sleepy tired as it was nearing 11 p.m. and I had been up since 3:30 a.m. Seeing all my friends really put a pep in my step.

"Let's go!" I said as I stepped onto the pavement with everyone. We started marching up Bath Road. Brad led the way keeping me moving quickly but not too fast. He did perfect pacing to move me forward and make up time on the way.

"How are you feeling?" Scott asked.

"I feel good!" I said. "I'm tired, but I'm so excited to see you all!"

As we hiked up the road, I told Brad my legs were killing me.

"Why don't you try walking backwards?" he offered.

I laughed. "I will just fall down, that's dumb." I had no filter on my words at this point. Thank goodness my crew and pacers were still putting up with me.

"Seriously, try it," Brad said. "I won't let you fall." I carefully turned around and started walking backwards uphill. Low and behold, Brad was right. It was easier and I could use my muscles differently. Brad led me up Bath Road and reminded me to hydrate and focus on putting one foot in front of (or should I say behind) the other. I talked about how the race had been so far and what was coming up next. Everyone asked me simple questions about the course, and how I was feeling. I could tell they were trying to keep my spirits light.

"Where's Carol?" I asked Joe.

"She's setting up our crew spot in Foresthill. She will be waiting for you when you arrive," Joe responded.

As we neared the top of Bath Road, I carefully turned around to walk forward again. From Bath Road, the course continues along a worn dirt path right beside Foresthill Road for about a mile as runners drop into the town of Foresthill. We made the left from Bath Road onto the dirt path and started running.

I was so pumped I started running pretty fast, while still talking to everyone about the race.

"Whoa runner," Brad said as he ran right beside me. "You're taking this section way too fast. Let's dial it back and cruise in easy. No need to burn all your energy."

"Oh!" I said with a giggle. "Sorry Brad. I'm just so amped to get to Foresthill!"

Everyone laughed with me. They couldn't believe I was so positive, or maybe delirious this far into the race.

"You are doing awesome!" Scott said excitedly.

"Thanks Scott! This is so cool!" I replied.

"I've been waiting to get to run this portion with you," he said with a giant smile.

We trotted along the path following the road into Foresthill. About a quarter mile out I could hear the buzz of the aid station and see the flood lights illuminating the street.

Foresthill was one of the busiest aid stations of the entire race. It's located at mile 62 and is the first location you can pick up a pacer if it's still light outside. After about 8pm, you are able to pick up a pacer in Michigan Bluff as I did. Foresthill also is the easiest aid station to get to and has plenty of parking. As you leave the aid station, you travel down Main Street (which parallels Foresthill Road) for about half a mile through town before you make your way back onto the dirt trail. It's a great location to spectate the leaders coming through earlier in the day and really take in everything that's happening. As you come into Foresthill, 200 yards before the aid station, the path turns into asphalt along the main road.

We continued to trot along the path coming into the aid station.

"Laura!" I heard someone scream. "You look amazing!!"

I glanced up straight ahead of me and saw two of my co-workers, Diane and Eric, standing on the other side of the barrier.

"Hi guys!" I yelled back as I ran towards them. The barriers funnel runners and pacers to the left while any crew or team members running in with you funnel to the right. I ran directly into the arms of Diane and a welcomed hug as my crew and friends funneled to the right towards the other end of the aid station.

"Oh my gosh, Laura," she said. "You look so good! You're doing so great!"

"Thank you!" I said as she let me go.

"Hi, Eric!" I said as I hugged him. "Thank you both for coming out. It's great to see you!"

"We wouldn't miss it!" they replied. "Get going! You're doing great!"

"Let's move Laura," Brad said as he gently guided me towards the aid station check in.

I walked into the aid station, "1-2-6 in!" I yelled.

"That's the spirit!" one volunteer yelled back at me.

"Are these salt tabs?" I asked as I saw a bowl of white pills.

"They are," a volunteer responded.

"SCaps or Endurolytes?" I asked.

"SCaps," they said.

"Great thanks!" I replied as I grabbed one and popped it in my mouth. While I had been drinking my electrolytes throughout the day, I knew I was behind a bit on them and wanted to be sure I had plenty of electrolytes in my system to avoid cramping as I went into the overnight hours.

"Can I get some Coke?"

"Here you go!" a volunteer replied as she handed me a paper cup of soda. "There are quesadillas up ahead and soup too."

"Thanks! Brad, I want some soup," I said as I made my way down the table. I peered up and he already had soup and a quesadilla in his hand waiting for me. "You're the best Brad," I said.

"Let's go. Your crew is set up just down the street," he replied.

"OK. You guys rock!" I yelled back towards the tents as we walked out of the aid station. "1-2-6 out!"

My crew was set up on the right-hand side of the street about 100 feet from the end of the aid station. Carol had everything laid out in the back of our SUV when I walked up. Candie, Karyn and a few others had shown up to wish me luck too!

"Hi everyone!" I said. I was so happy to see more smiling faces.

"Give me your bottles," Joe said as he stepped toward me. I handed them and my knuckle light over and he proceeded to fill my bottles with everything I needed.

"Come over here," Carol said as I walked towards her. "Turn around," she insisted as she guided me to put my back to her. She began pulling trash out of my pack and refilling it with things I would need.

"Here's your inhaler. Take a few puffs," Carol instructed, and I did as I was told. With my sports-induced asthma, I planned to take puffs off my inhaler every 10-15 miles to keep my chest open and my breathing easy.

"Take a bite of this," Brad said, holding a quesadilla in front of my face. I grabbed it and bit a piece off.

"Who has my soup?" I asked. Brad handed me a cup. "Thanks." I began sipping the soup as Carol continued removing and adding gear to my pack. She took my neck cooler off and tossed it in the back of the car.

"Is my long sleeve in my pack?" I asked Carol.

"Yes, you've got everything," Carol said. "Joe, bottles."

"Here you go," Joe said as he handed both of my bottles to Brad and gave me my knuckle light. "You got this, honey," Joe told me with a smile as he gave me a quick kiss goodbye.

"You guys are so amazing!" I said gazing at my crew and friends. "Thank you again."

"Ready Brad?" I asked.

"Let's do this," he replied, as we started off down the street.

"How far to the next aid station?" I asked him.

"Cal-1 is in just under four miles," Brad replied. "You're fine. Just keep moving."

"How far off of the cutoff are we?"

"We got out of there with about 20 minutes to spare," he said. "Can you run?"

"Yup," I said. My goal was to be able to run from Foresthill on and luckily I had legs left. I finished my soup, tucked the cup in my pack and took my bottles from Brad, securing them to my hands with my light. We started jogging down Main Street towards the California Street turn.

"I know you're nervous and worried about finishing, but now I need you to focus on moving forward and nothing else until we get to the river, got it?"

"Ok. I can do that," I responded.

Main Street down to California Street is a gradual downhill and we took advantage, running at a good speed down the street. We easily took the left-hand turn onto California Street following it to the dead end and made a right onto Lowe Street. We followed the street as it turned left to where the road ends at Mosquito Ridge Road. We crossed the road and continued down the trail making our way out of Foresthill and into the canyon.

"Brad, how far off of the 30-hour time am I?" I asked, concerned.

"You're about 30 minutes behind it right now. We made up a little time in that section. But I don't want you to worry about that," he said confidently. "If we just keep moving we will make it just fine. The cutoffs get easier from here on out."

"Are you sure?" I asked. "I really want to finish this race."

"I know you do. Do you trust me?" he questioned.

"I do," I said confidently.

"Then stop asking questions and just keep running," he said with a laugh.

"Oh Brad," I said, laughing.

Despite the light-hearted banter, I couldn't help but feel like we wouldn't actually make it.

# TWELVE
June 6, 2008

While I had always been relatively healthy, college had helped me gain a solid amount of weight. I was four years into my post-college career and life in Sacramento, and was known to enjoy happy hour often and eating out with friends. I had belonged to gyms and gone for evening walks with one of my co-workers, but nothing had ever really helped me make a solid change in my life to lose the extra weight and get healthy. One day I decided it was time to make a commitment to a gym and get a personal trainer. My roommate at the time had worked with a personal trainer to lose weight, so I figured that would be a good idea for me too.

I walked into the gym after work on a Friday. I joined the Gold's Gym in my neighborhood as it checked off all of my requirements. It was near my home, I could go do cardio after work and it was reasonably priced. I liked this gym because the cardio equipment was up on the second floor, where the serious weight lifters couldn't see me working out. I was a shy gym-goer back then. I didn't even know how to use the weights, much less want to step foot near all those guys grunting and sweating all over the equipment. Yuck!

I walked myself right upstairs and hopped on the first elliptical machine. I loved to burn through a 45- to 60-minute elliptical workout. I'd get a good heart rate increase and feel like I had gotten in a run, even if I hadn't set foot on the pavement or treadmill.

In July of the previous year I had started running after Cathy's accident. That October I ran my first "real" 5K as part of my training. After a few other shorter races, I had worked my way up to 10 miles completing the Big Sur 10 Miler (part of the Big Sur Marathon event) in April 2008. That was such a grand goal for me -- and my first inclination that I was really ready to start marathon training.

So, on this day, I walked into the gym and went straight to the cardio floor, but in my heart, I knew that's not why I was here. I was here to make a personal training appointment. I know, me, on the weight floor with all these sweaty people? No way! When I signed up for my membership, the sales guy had told me that it came with a free personal training session with whichever trainer I wanted. The trainer would discuss my goals and teach me how to use the equipment properly. And if I liked it, I could sign up for a personal training package with that trainer or someone else. I had decided there was no time like the present to add some conditioning to my running program. And I was hoping I could lose 10-20 pounds to help make running easier.

After I pumped through my elliptical workout, I went over to the stretching area to do some abs exercised and build up the courage to go talk to a trainer. It took me about 20 minutes to do so, but I finally walked down the stairs from the cardio floor and headed for the trainer area.

There was a gigantic fellow sitting at the desk working on some paperwork. I walked up as he raised his head and smiled at me.

"Hi," I said.

"Hello there!" he replied. "How can I help you?"

"I just joined the gym and the guy who sold me my membership told me I could do a free session with you guys to learn the equipment?" I spurted out as fast as I could.

He gave a chuckle and said, "Sure thing." He extended his hand to me. "I'm Elijah."

I put my hand in his giving a firm shake and replied, "I'm Laura. I'm not usually this nervous."

"It's completely understandable," Elijah said. "Have you ever had a trainer before?"

"No. Never really considered it," I replied sheepishly.

"OK. No worries!" he replied, clearly excited at the prospect of training a newbie like me. "What day of the week works best for you?"

I started to think through my calendar for the week. "Any evening after 6 really works."

"How about this coming Monday at 6 p.m.?" he asked.

"That'll be great!" Surprisingly, I started to get enthusiastic for this new adventure. I think Elijah's positivity was rubbing off on me. He took my name and cell phone number, adding my appointment to his calendar.

"Awesome. Meet me here at the desk at 6," he instructed. "If you can get here about 10 minutes early, hop on the cardio equipment for a warm up, then meet me down here."

"Will do," I replied. "Thanks Elijah."

I bounced away from the trainers' desk feeling excited and optimistic for my first training session.

◆ ◆ ◆

The next morning, I woke up early and had a quick breakfast. It was the first day of my first season running with Sacfit, a local running group training for the California International Marathon (CIM) coming up in December. When I started running the year before, my big goal was to cross the finish line at CIM. I had spent the previous 11 months training alone and decided to join a training group for marathon training. My friend Megan ran with Sacfit and had finished her first marathon using the Galloway Method, also known as a run/walk method. It uses timed intervals to run and walk through the entire length of a workout or race. When she explained the run/walk method, it actually made running a marathon seem manageable. With her guidance, I was now up to running a five minute run, one minute walk interval for my training.

I drove down to William B. Pond Park along the American River Parkway. I quickly found the group near the 13.5 mile marker on the trail and checked in. I saw a couple ladies standing together and thought they looked friendly, so I walked over and introduced myself.

"Hi there, I'm Laura," I said and put my hand out to the first gal.

"Hey," she replied as she took my hand. "I'm Trista."

"Nice to meet you," I replied.

"What pace do you run?" I asked. "I'm about a 12-minute per mile runner. And I run five minutes and walk one minute."

"That's about what I run," Trista replied.

"Great! We should run together!" I offered.

"Sounds good."

The group director, Ken, called our attention over the loud speaker. He let us know we would be running a pace run today, which would provide us with a baseline for our pace groups. Ken instructed us to run two miles, one mile out and back, at a moderate pace. We were asked to take our heart rate when we got back and time our run as well. He sent us out in groups along the trail and had other coaches waiting for us to help with heart rates when we got back.

When Trista and I returned from our two-mile pace run, we recorded our times and heart rates, then handed in our paperwork. We made plans to meet up again the next Saturday if we ended up in the same pace group and went on our way. As I walked back to my car, I thought about how fun this was going to be since I had already made a friend to run with. I had been nervous going into the training, but also felt pretty good about it since I had already run a 10-miler.

♦ ♦ ♦

That next Monday, I left work at 5 p.m. and arrived at the gym about 5:40 p.m. I changed my clothes in the locker room, locked up my bags and headed to the cardio floor. I hopped on an elliptical to get in a quick warm-up per Elijah's instructions the Friday before. A few minutes before 6 p.m., I stepped off the machine and made my way down to the trainers' desk where Elijah was waiting for me.

"Hey there! Ready to go?" he asked as I walked up.

"Yup! Just got in 10 minutes on the elliptical," I replied.

"I saw you head up there," Elijah said. "Glad you got that in first. Let's go!" He escorted me onto the weight floor and I automatically felt nervous.

*What am I doing here?* I asked myself. *This is not where I belong. I sure hope he teaches me everything so I don't look like an idiot out here.*

Elijah showed me around the weight floor, moving around the huge guys and fit women. I automatically felt uncomfortable and out of place, pulling on my workout clothes nervously and staring down at the floor.

*I hope someday I will be able to work out like those women,* I thought to myself. *That would be amazing! There's no way I could do that right now.*

Elijah took me through a full-body workout, alternating between the machines and free weights. He explained how each machine worked and what it did to that body part and muscle. To my surprise I found it all extremely interesting. Maybe because I'm a hands-on learner, but the whole "lifting weights thing" started to connect with me.

By halfway through the workout (and what felt like my 500th round of squats), I was already feeling like I could barely move. But one thing I noticed was how much energy I was feeling coursing through my body. I knew exercise released endorphins, but this was fantastic!

"You're doing really great," Elijah complimented. "How are you feeling?"

"I'm hanging in there," I replied. "I may not be able to walk tomorrow though!" I said with a laugh.

He laughed and said, "You will be fine. I can already tell."

We discussed my goals, what my marathon training would look like over the next six months and what I wanted to get from weight training. Elijah also asked me about my diet and work out schedule. We chatted about our families and how he came to be a personal trainer. I also told him about Cathy and why I chose to run a marathon.

I felt a real connection with Elijah immediately. He made me feel smart and empowered, and felt like a friend. I'm sure all trainers "sell" like that because they want you to feel like they are your best friend. I didn't care. It was a great feeling to have someone who didn't treat me like I wasn't smart since I was new to weight lifting.

We went through a few more exercises then he took me over to the stretching area and ran me through an ab routine with crunches, twists and even a few planks. When we were done he helped me up off the floor.

"Oh my gosh, I'm going to die!" I said.

Elijah laughed. "You are not going to die," he said. "You did great! So what do you think? Want to try this on your own or do you want to do some personal training?"

"I've got to schedule some sessions with you," I replied. "I need this for sure!"

"Great! Let's check out the calendar and I can tell you about packages." Elijah walked me back to the trainers' desk and showed me the packages. I signed up for a 10-session package right there and we scheduled my next session for that Thursday. We would start with two sessions a week, and one workout a week for me to do by myself. Then we would cut it back to one a week with two sessions a week for me by myself.

That Thursday we met and started by taking my measurements and body fat so we obtained a baseline for my progress. Elijah told me we would take new measurements each month so we could see any changes, including how much body fat I had lost.

Elijah started me with a push-pull workout and on my days alone and gave me some assigned exercises he wanted me to do. The first training session would be push, where I would do all the exercises that require you to push away from the body (chest press, leg press, shoulder press, etc.). The next training session would be pull, where I pull towards the body (seated row, hamstring curl, bicep curl, etc.). On the last day I did a lot of bodyweight exercises and some machines he assigned to me.

Elijah also gave me a daily calorie goal and information about nutrition so I could start working on my diet. I decided to go all in on the diet portion. I started eating eggs and turkey bacon for breakfast, with a protein shake for snack. Then lunch was a salad or sandwich, but I measured everything and packed it myself. My afternoon snack was a protein bar and then dinner was something simple. Before long runs I would have pasta, and other nights I would have lean meats and salad.

Over the first four weeks training with Elijah, carrying out my marathon training plan and following the healthier eating guidelines, I lost 10 pounds! Mind you, I was eating pretty terrible before that. Often I would eat fast food or pizza for dinner and a donut and fancy coffee drink for breakfast. And lunch was almost always a microwave meal with a yogurt and a candy bar. I barely ate meat because I just didn't want to make the effort to cook something difficult. No wonder I couldn't lose weight. I was eating horribly — and way too much! I had gone from a size 12/14 to a size 10 in that first month. I felt great!

Running was ticking up and I was working towards my first half marathon – the Disneyland Half Marathon. I was getting nervous about it, but I felt strong since I had lost some weight and was really enjoying all of my training. I continued to push myself through the summer and ran my first half marathon Labor Day weekend 2008. My 2:45 time was right around where I wanted to be for the race, and I knew I could go into the rest of my training and do well.

As I continued to work out with Elijah in the gym, I began to feel much stronger when running. I continued to lose weight and found my groove on longer runs. Over the next few months as the mileage grew, I started to feel more fit and ready to take on my first full marathon.

Six months later in November, I was still training with Elijah two days a week and getting in my runs. It was a lot on my calendar, combined with my full-time job and then boyfriend, but I knew if I worked hard I would get to my goal. And I couldn't let my goal of running for Cathy fall by the wayside either.

I got in my last 8-mile run the weekend before the marathon and I was feeling great! I hadn't been very good at foam rolling during my training, so I dealt with some IT band issues, but I cleared those up and was ready to take on this huge goal. When December rolled around I toed the line at the CIM. I was now 15 pounds lighter than when I started training with Elijah, with more muscle mass and a ton more confidence. I was ready to kill the race!

With my Sacfit running tribe beside me, I ran my first marathon in 5:56. It was slower than I had hoped, but I finished – and that's what mattered to me. I crossed the line with my parents, brother, godparents and boyfriend looking on. It was an amazing feeling to achieve a goal I never thought I would.

They say right after a marathon, you swear you will never run it again. Then about two weeks later you'll most likely sign up for another one. Before my post-marathon two weeks were up, I had already signed up for my second marathon, the San Francisco Marathon in June 2009.

◆ ◆ ◆

From that point forward, I became a running and fitness addict. I started with a goal to run a marathon in every state. I checked off California, then Hawaii (Big Island International Marathon - 2010), then Illinois (Chicago Marathon - 2010), and Tennessee (Nashville Country Music Marathon - 2011). I did the San Francisco Marathon again that year. Soon after that, our running group started an Ultramarathon training program. Kelly and I debated joining but ultimately decided we would wait until the next year to try anything crazy, because those ultra-runners were *obviously* nuts. I continued to train with Sacfit and paced the runners from our training group at the CIM in 2011.

I was also still training with Elijah and spending extra time getting in my own workouts at the gym. I loved my new fit life and how much I had grown since making this change for myself. I had been a cheerleader growing up, but this took my fitness to a whole new level. I felt like a solid athlete now.

It was early 2012 when Kelly and I were asked to pace fellow Sacfit runners at the American River 50 Mile Endurance Run (AR50). I had never run trails and didn't know what I was doing, but I figured I would be OK to pace my friend. Kelly and I decided to run some trails just to get a feel for what we would be up against pacing people.

We got to see some picturesque sights and figured it wouldn't be so bad to run the trails. Ultimately we paced our friends for 15 miles and loved every single minute of it!

After that, I started running trails with friends. Short distances to start, then I got the bug. I decided to abandon my goal of 50 marathons in 50 states and start running trail races instead. While running in every state would have been fun, there was something about solitude in the mountains that made my heart happier than it had ever been while running. Thus began my love affair with ultra-distance running.

I have to be honest. I ran my first ultra-distance 50K in November 2009 well before I started my ultramarathon career. There was a 50K that ran on the American River Parkway, which is a 31-mile, paved trail from Folsom to Sacramento. Kelly, Trista and I decided that since it was on our training course and we knew the route, we would do it. We figured a 50K was only five more miles than a marathon so why not? We finished and felt accomplished, but I have to say there's nothing like running a 50K or further in the mountains. It's just... different.

As I continued to immerse myself in the running community, I got the opportunity to volunteer at the Western States Endurance Run with a group of running friends. In June 2012, we worked at the Rucky Chucky River Crossing. I directed runners down to the river from the road for the 10 p.m.-6 a.m. shift. What an experience! I got to see my coach, Ken, come through on his way to the finish. That year, I also went to the finish line and ran Ken into the stadium when he finished Western States. I was elated for him and felt the buzz of the ultra-running community. It was electric!

I joined the Sacfit Ultra training group towards the end of 2012 and ran my first trail 50K at Way Too Cool in March 2013. That same year, I ran my first 50 miler at the AR50 in April. I was so hooked! I wanted to run trails all the time. Every single chance I got, I wanted to get my feet dirty.

It was after that first 50 miler that I had "the" conversation with my coach, Ken.

"You're going to run 100 miles," he said to me.

"You are insane!" I laughed.

"You've got the talent, drive and determination. You can do it," Ken said energetically.

"I think you may be losing your mind," I chuckled, and shrugged off the whole conversation. There was NO WAY was I going to ever run 100 miles.

That month I got a job working at Fleet Feet Sacramento selling shoes and other merchandise. I loved living in the running world all the time. It made my heart happy. I met so many ultra-runners who had run 50K, 50 miles, 100 miles and more, including my future pacer Bob. We talked all about how exciting the experience was, especially when Western States was right in our backyard.

Fleet Feet Sacramento was in charge of the Ford's Bar aid station (mile 73) at Western States. With that aid station came a spot in the race for one runner from Fleet Feet Sacramento. The runner had to qualify for the race, and assist with Fleet Feet's Western States responsibilities. Then he or she could receive the spot if chosen among all of the qualified runners. In Summer 2013, I assisted as our team prepared to man the aid station for the long weekend in June. After seeing everything that went into it, and having volunteered previously at the race, I decided to try and qualify myself. I had no idea if I would pull it off, but I figured if there was no time like the present to try and take on this historic race.

◆ ◆ ◆

I signed up for the Javelina Jundred coming up in November 2014 as my qualifying race. It was a looped course in the Arizona desert and seemed like it would be something I could accomplish to get my qualifier. Bob was also planning to run the race to qualify for his chance at the Fleet Feet Sacramento spot.

I started my 100-mile season by training for Way Too Cool and AR50 again. I ate very healthy for the first part of 2014 and was able to drop 10 pounds that I had put on, bringing me to a great racing weight. The result garnered faster times at both races. I ran a personal best at Way Too Cool coming in 20 minutes faster than the previous year, and I beat my previous AR50 time by a full hour. I couldn't believe how well I was running, and I had high hopes for the rest of 2014.

In May 2014, I attempted my first 100K as a part of my training for Javelina Jundred. I started the race strong and ready, but got lost in the first 50K and ended up bruising my foot with a misstep on the trail. I made it into the halfway mark one second under the cutoff. I know – that one hurt! In a flurry of movement, my crew and pacer, Malia, got my things together and met me out on the trail. Sadly, I couldn't run much after that and had to throw in the towel at mile 40. It was my first DNF (did not finish) ever. While it was a blow to my ego, I knew that it was all part of the learning process of trail running. You have to go through the hard times to make the highs seem that much better.

Later that year I ran the Run on the Sly 50K with my future crew member Andy, and then the Overlook 50-mile race. I performed well at both races. I didn't realize that the Overlook 50-mile race ended up being a bit of a trial run for Western States. My crew chief, Carol, took the reins in crewing me, and my pacer Brad helped me run the last 15 miles.

It was around this time that Bob told me he had decided not to try to qualify for Western States that year. The Fleet Feet Sacramento spot was mine for the taking. I just had to qualify. That sure put pep in my step for the rest of my training!

I was ready for my first 100 miler and excited to take it on. I had lined up Malia, one of my AR50 pacers and crew, to go down to Arizona with me, as well as her sister Annie. I had been heat training by running in the middle of the afternoons in the scorching 102-degree weather. I felt like it was helping me acclimate to the desert heat I would experience in Arizona. I would also ride home from work in my hot car without the air conditioning on. I'd sweat and sip ice water. It was like sauna training, but I didn't have to pay for it!

In November, Malia and I made the trek down a few days early and met up with Annie in Tucson. The next day, we drove about 2.5 hours away to McDowell Mountain Regional Park in Fountain Hills, AZ. After we arrived, we headed to the Expo to check in and get my bib and goodie bag. While we were there we saw my buddy Brad who was also running the race. We headed to the park to meet my other friend Andrea and get set up in our tent where we would camp that night.

Andrea, who I had done many of my long training runs with, had saved us a tent near hers. We unpacked the car and then headed to meet my friend Rich for dinner. We all had a lot of nervous energy pent up and I was hoping being away from the campground would help us relax a little. We enjoyed a delicious meal, and of course, talked too much about the race. When we got back to the park I went over the last-minute details with Malia and Annie, and talked through race strategy with Rich.

This was it. I was about to run my first 100 miler ever. What was I thinking? Let's just say I barely slept that night.

The morning came quick. We got up, got dressed and walked to the start line. I took photos with Andrea, Brad and my crew, and then we were off. The day started cool but ended up very hot. The Javelina Jundred is a runnable course with only 700 feet of elevation gain per loop. It can be a quick race, but the heat can also lead to a runner's demise if they don't manage it well. I was very lucky that my body tolerates heat better than the cold.

Each loop switched directions, so I passed Rich several times while we were out there. We would always stop and hug, check in on how we were feeling, and keep on running. I also got to see Brad and Andrea out there throughout the race.

I saw my crew at the end of each loop in Javelina Jeadquarters, which upped my energy each time. I was so excited to pick up Malia on my first pacer loop at mile 45. She kept me going into the night until she switched with her sister for another night loop.

As we came into the morning, Malia joined me for the last long loop. I was dragging at this point, but she kept me moving. Malia was always motivating, encouraging me to run and helping me get whatever I needed at each aid station. At that point we had been friends for 29 years, so I can say she knew me really well.

One thing I had told my crew/pacers before the race was that I wasn't allowed to quit. If I even talked about quitting, I was to be sent right back out on the trail with a swift kick to my butt. I knew I had a Western States spot waiting for me, I just had to qualify to get it. There was NOTHING that would make me quit that race.

On my way back to headquarters on my sixth loop, I ran into Andrea at an aid station. We hugged and started crying. The sun was finally up and we could see the day was going to be better. Andrea was on her final loop and just had to finish to get her buckle.

"Go get that buckle!" I told her as we parted ways, wiping happy tears from our eyes.

The last loop is a shorter nine-miler that Annie did with me. I kept telling her that I was going to die out there and she finally told me to suck it up and run. Annie was such a great friend, but also tough pacer. Just who I needed by my side when I wanted to quit at 27 hours in.

Running in the last part of the loop was magical. Several friends including Brad, Tim and Kathleen, were waiting for me as I ran over the last undulation into the finish area. I was doing it! I was finishing my first 100 miler and I was going to get that Western States spot! I came into the finish and yelled Malia's name. She was waiting, camera ready to capture the moment for me.

As I crossed the finish in 28 hours and 10 minutes, they handed me my buckle and congratulated me on a job well done. I had done it! I ran 100 miles. I had done something I NEVER thought I would do in my life. It wasn't a race without drama though. I fell several times, ran into horrible digestion issues, and had to punt my fueling on many occasions. It wasn't the prettiest finish, but it was mine. And that was what mattered.

After finishing the race, Malia took a photo of me beaming with my buckle at the finish line. I quickly texted it to Pat and Jan, the owners of Fleet Feet Sacramento, to show them I had done it. The next text I received read, "Next up, Western States!" I had the spot. And I was elated!

After a shower and a hot meal, Annie took Malia and I to the airport and headed home herself. We flew home with Andrea and her crew, and Malia drove us all back to Sacramento. It was an adventure that allowed me the opportunity to toe the line at Western States. I had never felt like I was good enough to run anything that long or that tough, but I proved myself wrong. I proved that I could do anything I put my mind to.

♦♦♦

When you look at your life and wonder what you are going to do with it, do you choose the easy path? Or the hard one? Do you take the road well worn or the road less traveled? Do you push yourself or stay comfortable?

For me, running has pushed me to do things that make me uncomfortable all the time. It has given me the confidence to reach for higher goals in every part of my life. It has offered up a community that understands my kind of crazy, and supports me no matter what I choose to do. Running has imparted the ability to never say no, but to instead ask, "I wonder what I could do with that?"

I'm so glad I walked into that gym so many years ago and met Elijah. I'm grateful that I showed up at that first Sacfit workout and introduced myself to Trista. Those moments kicked off a part of my life that I never would have experienced had I not just decided to put doubt aside and try.

Taking care of your body takes care of your mind. Being willing to reach outside of your comfort zone will give you opportunities to see what you can do outside of your current bubble. Taking on new things makes you a stronger person. In 100 miles, you are outside of your comfort zone constantly. Whether it's a pace you don't want to run or an issue with your food that you have to try and figure out, you have to deal with the issues that may arise and the uncertainty of the race.

Running and getting fit taught me that even if you don't think you're an athlete, or a runner… you can be. You just have to believe it. And no matter what, if you keep putting one foot in front of the other, you will eventually get to the finish line.

# THIRTEEN
## Saturday, June 27, 2015 – Mile 62 - 11:25 p.m.

As Brad and I left Foresthill and began our descent down the switchbacks towards the bottom of the canyon, you could feel the night air seeping in, cool on your cheeks but not cold. We came down the single track and made a sweeping left onto the fire road, continuing down the mountain. I looked up and couldn't help but notice how brilliant the stars were in the dark sky. The fire road allowed for an amazing view of the sky with the trees set back from the trail.

*This is unreal,* I thought to myself. *I am so lucky to be out here!*

We made a right-hand turn down another fire road following the Western States flags. As we continued on the trail and made our way onto the single track, I started to slow. It was so dark and I was feeling really sleepy. Brad led the way but I know he could tell I was starting to get really groggy.

"You're doing great," he said.

"I'm so tired, Brad," I reacted quietly.

"Laura," he replied sternly. "I just need you to follow my feet and I will get you there. And Bob will get you to the finish."

"I know. I'm coming," I said.

*How in the world am I going to finish this thing when I'm this tired?* I thought to myself. *This is insane. I want to nap so bad.* I was hitting a low point in my race, and I was starting to question all of my abilities.

Every time you run a race, there will be lows. Earlier in my race I felt the fear of not being able to finish due to time. But this was different. I was starting to question if I'd be able to stay awake or have the energy to actually finish this race.

We made our way along the first set of long switchbacks towards a creek at the bottom of the mini-canyon. The switchbacks led us down along the single track through the dense, tree-lined forest. Brad took the lead as we approached the small creek. It was only a few feet wide, but we still needed to be careful with our footing as both sides were a bit steep.

As I went to step on a rock, my feet slid out from under me and I landed on my butt. I put my hands down on my bottles as I fell to break my stumble.

"Well, that's my third fall of the race," I laughed. "And you have been there for the last two!"

"You OK?" he asked, sounding concerned.

"Yeah, I'm totally fine, just tired and not moving as steadily as I was."

He took my hand and helped me up and across the creek.

"Let's go," I said.

The single track climbed back up and continued along with the canyon on our left and the mountain on our right.

Eventually some areas opened up and we could see the stars again. The air was quiet except for the pitter-patter of our feet as we made our way down the trail. We hadn't seen another runner in a long time. As time passes, runners spread further and further apart as their paces slowed down. So we were only seeing other runners and pacers when we reached some of the aid stations.

After a little while of running in silence I heard Brad ask, "You good?"

"Yup," I replied. I didn't have the energy to give much more of a response than that. I kept chugging along the trail maintaining my pace and space between my head lamp and Brad's feet.

"Every step forward is one step closer to the finish and one step further from a cutoff," I whispered out loud. "I got this."

"What the heck is that?" I heard Brad say.

I looked up ahead past him with my headlamp and saw a glow in the distance. As we grew closer, we saw glow sticks hanging from the trees and bushes lining the trail. Then we were able to make out the glow we saw past them.

"Are those aliens?" I asked Brad with a giggle.

"They seem to be!" He replied with a laugh. "Those are crazy looking!"

I started chuckling as we ran by inflatable glow-in-the-dark aliens that looked like they were two to three feet tall hanging in the trees. "That's enough to cause some serious hallucinations," I said.

"We must be close to Cal-1," Brad said.

Cal-1 was the Dardanelles Aid Station at about mile 65. The 15-mile section of the race from Foresthill to the river crossing at Rucky Chucky is known as the Cal Street or the Cal Loop section. There were three aid stations in this section before you reached the bottom of the canyon at the river crossing.

We started to hear noise ahead as we neared the aid station.

"We're almost there," Brad observed. "Have them fill your bottles. What do you want me to grab?"

"Soup and Coke," I replied. "You can count on me wanting soup and Coke every aid station from here on out."

"You got it," Brad said as we came up to the aid station. "1-2-6 in."

The Dardanelles aid station was on a wide turn in the single track, but the aid station itself was on a very small area. The pop-up tents were set up over the trail with the tables filling half of the space leaving a several foot wide area for runners and pacers to move through. There were chairs at the far end and volunteers all around waiting to help us with whatever we needed.

"Hi there!" the aid station volunteer said. "What can I do for you?"

"Can you fill this one bottle with water and one baggie of the powder in the handheld pouch?" I asked, handing them my bottle and tucking my second bottle under my left arm.

"Sure thing!" they said.

"Here's some soup and Coke," Brad said, holding out two cups.

"Thanks," I replied and started drinking the soup quickly. The aid station volunteers who made the soup cooled it down so we could actually drink it quickly without burning our faces off.

Every aid station has someone either checking runners in, or checking runners out, and sometimes both. This aid station had a volunteer waiting to check me out at the end of the food tables.

"You're doing great!" she said as she sat in a camping chair under a blanket. It was chilly for volunteers who weren't able to move around the way we were.

"How many miles to Cal-2?" I asked her.

"You have about five miles to go," the volunteer replied with a smile. "You have a little over an hour and a half before the cutoff," she said as she checked her watch. "Keep moving and you'll get there."

"She will get there," I heard Brad say as he came up behind me with another cup of soda and my filled handheld. "Let's go," he ordered.

I finished my soup, drank the cup of Coke I had in my hand and threw away the empty cups.

"Thank you all!" I shouted and quickly took the second cup of Coke Brad handed to me, downing the contents before we walked out of the aid station. Brad stepped onto the trail in front of me, handed me my bottle and we were off towards the finish once again. I carefully secured both bottles to my hands with my knuckle light as we began walking.

We were about 43 minutes behind the 30-hour time at Cal-1. It would take some serious work to make up the lost time and get ahead of the 30-hour to make it to the finish.

"I'll do whatever you tell me to do Brad," I begged. "The pain will be so much worse if I don't get a buckle." I knew I was starting to sound like a broken record, but the only thing I could think about was making it to the finish line in time.

"I know. Follow my feet," He said, demanding, but not harsh.

*Right foot, left foot,* I thought as we ran over rocks and cracks in the dirt. We moved along at a quick clip down the single-track trail. At this point my legs were starting to ache from the mileage. By the end of an ultra, everything hurts, so I knew this was par for the course, but I didn't expect to be so sore at mile 65.

*I know this part,* I thought, obviously feeling more energy from the soup and soda. *I know this so well.* I thought back to my 50-mile training run with Ken on Western States training weekend. We had killed this section. I had moved efficiently and didn't stop running on the gradual uphills. I remembered Ken telling me I was doing so great because I just kept going no matter what. Ken reminded me that I ran even when I could have taken a break to walk.

"Time to do that again, Laura," I said to myself. "Time to use that Granny Gear and just keep pushing forward."

We went a short way and came upon one of my least favorite climbs. It's a gradual uphill that turns steep as it moves up a few long switchbacks. These are the kind of climbs that feel like they will never end after they start.

When we started up the beginning of the hill, Brad marched up like a man on a mission. I obediently followed his footsteps forcing myself to move fast. My shins were still hurting from the walking miles back in the race. While the Tylenol had taken the edge off, they were starting to get aggravated again.

*Push through your glutes, Laura. Just like you practiced.* I thought. *You've done this part of the trail tons of times. You got this.*

The trail goes up, straight ahead then makes a sharp left continuing straight up in the first of three large switchbacks. At the top of the first one, it cuts sharply to the right, to parallel the first switchback up the mountainside for what feels like forever. The switchbacks on this section are so close together that it makes you feel like you're barely climbing the side of the mountain, especially in the dark. At the top of the second one, the trail cuts sharply back to the left continuing to parallel the switchback up further until it drops down to a flat and slight downhill.

"This is so hard," I whined to Brad between breaths.

"Keep going," he said, breathless himself.

*Left foot, right foot. Use the glutes,* I repeated in my head.

When we finally reached the top, Brad started running again. I wished he would just walk and give me a break, but he wouldn't. And I didn't have time to spare to do that.

*I have to keep my eye on the prize and keep moving forward.* I thought. *There's no room for error here.*

We rolled through the skinny single-track trail with ease. Down the downhills, continuing to run the gradual ups.

"You with me?" I heard Brad ask.

"Yup," I replied breathless.

"Are you drinking?" he asked.

"Yes," I replied and took a drink of my Skratch.

*I need to keep drinking,* I told myself as I took another sip.

I looked up with my headlamp and saw the Manzanita bushes in the distance on the trail.

*We're here,* I thought. I knew we were coming up on "Elevator Shaft," as we call it. It's a short section of the trail that's so steep downhill that it feels like you're going down an elevator. It's full of slippery rocks and can be tough to navigate on the way down, plus it pushes your quads to the limit late in the race.

"We're at Elevator Shaft," Brad hollered at me. "Take it easy. Let's make it through this without any incidents."

"Good idea," I replied calmly.

We began the descent down elevator shaft slowly, taking the slippery parts careful and making sure we planted our feet well. There was no reason to get hurt trying to take this part too fast.

We made it through the hardest part of the descent and started trotting down again, still watching our footing. Elevator shaft continued down for what seemed like forever until we got to a semi-flat area and started running again. We cruised along with Brad continuing to remind me to drink water and eat my fuel.

"Peachstone should be right up here," Brad said. Peachstone was the Cal-2 aid station. The aid station space was a huge area with several cots, Christmas lights hanging overhead and tons of volunteers. Of the aid stations in the Cal Street section, it was the easiest location to take dropped runners out of the race course because the access road went directly into the aid station.

We ran along with the canyon wall on our right and the drop off to our left. Through the trees I could see the lights from the Peachstone aid station. There was music playing and a lot of chatter in the area. I was so happy to have finally reached another aid station.

"Hello runner!" the volunteers yelled as I came down the hill into the wide-open space.

"Hey!" I yelled back. Their energy was infectious. I slowed my pace to a walk as Brad went ahead of me to grab soup and another Coke. I looked to my right and there were several cots set up, a few of them being occupied by runners who were resting or not looking too well.

*Do I look like them?* I thought to myself. Just then Brad came up and grabbed my arm handing me a cup of soup.

"Drink this," he ordered. I tucked one of my bottles under my right arm, grabbed the cup and started sipping. "You're fine. Get what you need and we're out of here."

I walked to the table and asked the first volunteer to fill one of my handhelds with water and a pouch of Skratch powder as I had finished another 20 ounces of fluid. They ran off with my bottle as I moved to the food table. I grabbed a handful of Fritos Scoops and ate a few gummy bears between sips of soup.

"These gummy bears are delicious!" I laughed at one of the volunteers.

"Aren't they?" she said back to me. Brad came up next to me with a cup of soda. I finished my soup, handed him the cup and started drinking the soda right away.

"Thank you all for being here. You're so awesome." I was feeling so incredibly grateful for everyone out there helping us through this huge race. Western States has thousands of volunteers, from the aid stations to the start and finish lines, to the check in process at Squaw Valley the days before the race. It truly would not run as well as it does without the amazing volunteers there to help out.

After a few seconds Brad said, "Alright, we're ready to move." He was standing there patiently holding my filled water bottle. I stuffed a few Fritos in my mouth, finished my cup of soda, took my bottle from under my arm and the bottle from Brad and we headed towards the trail down the mountain.

"OK. Thanks again!" I called back to the volunteers as Brad led me down the wide path out of the Peachstone lights and back into the night.

*I hate the dark,* I thought as we made our way down the trail. *I hate the dark so much. There are so many sounds and scary things in the night.*

"How are you doing?" Brad asked as we trotted downhill from the aid station.

"I'm good," I replied laughing. I was beyond delirious at this point.

At Peachstone I had made up a lot of time on the 30-hour mark. I was now only 20 minutes behind 30-hour pace.

"Keep moving. Follow my feet. Next stop is Ford's Bar where all our friends are!" he said excitedly.

"Really? Oh Yay!" I replied, equally excited. I had gotten my spot in the race on the Ford's Bar aid station volunteer spot. It's run by Fleet Feet Sacramento, and staffed by volunteers who were employees, coaches and runners from the training programs, so I knew I would see all of our friends at the aid station. "I can't wait to see everyone!" Many of our friends had told me prior to the race that they would be working the overnight shift so they could see me come through.

"How many miles until we're there?" I asked.

"It's only a couple miles," Brad replied.

We followed the downhill single track among the groves of tall trees. The dirt was well packed and smooth as we coasted downhill. The trail was wider as you left Peachstone and slowly slimmed down with the canyon on the left-hand side. There were a few switchbacks on our way down to the river's edge. We followed them through sharp corners and eventually popped out from the single track onto the ranger road to begin the unrelenting climb up seven-minute hill.

"I hate seven-minute hill," I stated to Brad. "Like. Hate. It!" I emphasized.

"March up. That's all you can do. It's a seven-minute climb. Let's go!" he ordered.

We started hiking uphill, pushing with our legs and pumping our arms to help with efficiency. I began to lose my breath early in the hill. My legs and arms were pumping well, but the angle of the hill was much more than my breathing could handle at this point in the race. I kept pushing on up and as we approached the first plateau I knew I could take a short breather at the top.

As I began to slow I heard Brad say, "Don't even think of stopping. Keep your momentum going. We're almost there."

"I'm dying, Brad," I whined.

"I don't care. I know you aren't dying. Push Laura," he ordered. In this moment, I realized exactly why Brad was the right pacer for this section.

I was so mad at him. I started cussing. Dropping F-bombs between breaths and stomping my feet like a child. We made the right-hand turn at the plateau continuing uphill at the same pace. The trail continued up for about 30 yards ahead of us, then made a sharp left-hand turn and would continue uphill again for another 30 yards or so.

"One more turn and we are at the flat where it's all downhill to Ford's Bar," Brad said between breaths. "You got this, keep pushing and then we get to see our friends."

"I hate you, Brad," I said. He knew I didn't mean it, but it was the only sentence I could formulate in my breathless state. I was trying my best to stay positive, but it was so hard when I was so sleepy and physically spent.

"I know you do. We're almost there," Brad responded with a chuckle.

We took the left-hand turn and I could see the top of the last hill.

*I can do this,* I thought to myself. *I can. Believe, Laura. Just believe.*

And then like magic we were cresting the top and I had made it through seven-minute hill.

"We did it!" I yelled at Brad.

"See! I knew you would be fine!" he said. "Now let's get to Ford's Bar!"

"Can we walk for just a minute?" I asked.

"One minute," he replied. "Look over there. See that light through the trees? That's Ford's Bar and our friends."

"It is?" I replied, now excited. "Well, let's run then!"

Brad started doing our group's call across the canyon. "Ca-caw!" he yelled. "Ca-caw! Ca-caw!"

"Do you think they can hear us?" I asked.

"I can't hear them calling back so I'm guessing no," he said as we broke into a jog.

The trail descends down to the river along the ranger and rafting access road. It's an easy downhill with a few gradual rollers and it curves along the canyon. While we could see the light from the Ford's Bar aid station at Cal-3, it would still take us several minutes to get there. We picked up speed on the downhill and as we approached the last downhill, Brad started calling out to them again.

"Ca-caw, Ca-caw!" he yelled.

"WHOOOOO!!" we heard in response. "It's Laura!! She's coming!!" We heard them all start screaming.

I started screaming back to them as we ran down the hill into the light of the aid station. The music was pumping, the lights were on and everyone surrounded us when we came cruising in.

"How are you?"

"What do you need?"

Everyone was asking, ordering and working to get us in and out of the aid station. We got to see so many friends including Linda, John, Jeremy, Justin and a bunch of others.

Justin, the aid station captain, walked up and hugged me holding up a piece of quesadilla in front of me. "Eat this," he ordered. I tucked one of my bottles under my left elbow and diligently followed his orders eating the quesadilla. It tasted so good.

"You look great!" John said.

"You're making great time!" Linda yelled.

"Let's take a selfie!" Jeremy screamed, holding his cell phone up in front of us for a photo.

"Can I get some soup?" I asked as I finished the quesadilla. Almost immediately a cup of soup appeared in my hand. It was like I had a 10-person pit crew just for me!

"You guys are amazing!" I yelled. "It's so great to see all of you."

Brad walked up with a cup of soda. I balanced the soup on one hand with a handheld and drank the Coke right away. I handed him the cup and continued sipping the soup.

There was so much commotion around me that I didn't really know what was happening. Luckily Brad made sure to keep our friends calm and let me say hello to each of them before we got ready to leave the aid station.

I finished the soup, and handed the cup off. Then I grabbed some Fritos and Oreos from the food table and tucked them in the front pocket of my pack. I glanced over at Brad.

"Let's get out of here!" he said. "Sorry to eat and run guys!"

"No worries!"

"Get out of here!"

"Get her to the river Brad!" they all yelled.

Justin walked up, gave me a quick hug and a pat on the back as I adjusted my bottles and knuckle light. He handed me another piece of quesadilla for the road. "Get out of here," he said. "Go get that buckle!"

We walked out of the aid station down the single track so I could finish eating my food. The energy of all our friends at the aid station had us walking down the trail pretty quickly and feeling re-energized.

"That was amazing and crazy!" I said to Brad with a mouth full of quesadilla. "It was like they were all our crew!"

"They were," he replied. "I knew they would be."

Once I had finished my quesadilla and had some Fritos and Oreos, we started jogging along the river. The Ford's Bar aid station brings you about 30 feet above the river. As you head towards Rucky Chucky river crossing, the river is on your left and the cliffs are on your right. I knew the far side of Rucky Chucky was where I would get my next pacer, Bob. That was also where my crew would be waiting for us again. I couldn't be more excited to get to see them all.

Races like this take a toll on you not only physically, but mentally, especially at night. By now I had been running for about 22 hours. I started to hallucinate that tree stumps were bears, and shadows on the canyon wall were people climbing up the mountain. They weren't of course, but they sure looked like they were.

"Just keep running," Brad would say when I'd get quiet. "You got this. We have plenty of time to get to Rucky Chucky."

At Ford's Bar we didn't know how far I was behind the 30-hour pace, but Brad knew we had been moving well to get there so we kept our fingers crossed that we had made up time. We cruised along through the sandy parts of the trail as we dropped closer and closer to the river in the canyon.

We exited the single track and headed down the dirt ranger road towards the aid station. We knew there would be a couple of climbs before we got to Rucky Chucky so we took it easy as we moved along.

"I need to go to the bathroom," I said to Brad.

"Can you wait until we get to Rucky Chucky?" he asked.

"I have to wait. It's number 2," I said with a giggle. Everything was funny to me at this point of the race.

"Oh!" Brad said with a laugh. "Well, you can go out here, but if you can make it there it would be much better."

We shared a giggle and kept trotting along the road. As we neared the aid station, we could hear the noise of the music and volunteers. We could also see the lights down in the river.

The Rucky Chucky river crossing is a very large river crossing, unlike any other water crossing in the race. There's a cable stretched across the width of the river, secured on either side. There are volunteers standing in the water wearing wet suits to help make sure you get across safely. You wear a life vest and have to hold onto the cable the whole time as volunteers use glow sticks to point out large rocks and the best spots to place your feet.

The crossing is about 30 yards from shore to shore and takes some careful maneuvering. Many of the runners early in the race swim across while holding the cable so they can cool their bodies down. There's also a safety rafting boat to catch any runners who may let go of the cable and float downstream. Unfortunately, if helped by the boat, runners are automatically disqualified from the race.

As we came down the last hill into the aid station, the breadth of the set up came into focus. I had volunteered at this aid station years before and it appeared much different from the runner's point of view. There were several tents set up along the left side of the aid station near the river. Cars were parked along the right side of the parking lot up against the cliffs of the canyon.

I handed Brad my bottles and made a bee-line for the bathrooms over near the cars. Brad went to the aid station to refill my bottles since I hadn't filled them at Ford's Bar, and to get me soup and Coke. After I left the bathroom, I met Brad at the food tables.

"Hi there," I said.

"What can we help you with?" they asked as Brad handed me soup and Coke.

I held up the cups, "I think I'm good!" I said with a smile.

"How are you doing?" Brad asked, concerned.

"I'm good. I feel much better," I said.

I drank my soup and Coke and threw away the cups.

"I'm ready, let's do this," I said to Brad.

"OK, let's go!" he said excited. "We're crossing the river!"

"Bob is on the other side!" I said getting excited.

"He is for sure!" Brad said.

We made our way past the aid station to the start of the rock steps down to the river. The steps were not normal stairs. They were large steps, that each seemed to be 10-12 inches high. I'm sure they weren't that high but they sure felt like it after 78 miles of running.

"Who put these stairs here?" I yelled, laughing to the volunteers. "Don't they know I just ran 78 miles?"

I laughed as I made my way down the stairs to the water.

A volunteer yelled across the water, "Laura is coming across! Bib 1-2-6!"

That's when I heard it. Bob's voice.

"I'm here Laura!" he yelled across the water.

"Bob!" I screeched loudly. "I'm coming, Bob!"

I was so excited to be getting across the water to my next pacer, Bob.

*I'm closer to the finish now,* I told myself. *Bob is there, let's go!*

Brad and I made it to the bottom of the stairs where the volunteers were waiting.

"How deep is the deepest part of the water?" I asked.

"It can get about chest deep so if you have something in your pack you want to keep dry, move it higher," the volunteer said.

"I don't want my long sleeve to get wet. Can you pull it out of my pack and tie it around my neck?" I asked.

The volunteer pulled it out and tied it around my neck as another volunteer helped Brad into a life vest. They got me into one next and put a glow necklace around my neck to designate me as the runner, not a pacer. I tucked my handheld bottles in the front of my vest so I wouldn't lose them on the trek across.

"You ready?" Brad said.

"Let's go!" I yelled as we splashed into the frigid water.

# FOURTEEN
January 2004

Nearly six months before I was set to graduate, I had started to do research on where I wanted to move after classes ended at Chico State. I knew that I didn't want to stay in Chico – I wanted to do something big with my life, away from my small town. I was working on a minor in recording arts, so I had big dreams of working in the music industry in Los Angeles. My primary focus was record companies, but I also explored all of the public relations agencies I could find in Los Angeles and New York City.

I didn't get any bites for jobs when I got close to graduation, so I took a leap of faith and moved to NYC with a friend who had gone to college there. I spent a lot of time applying for jobs and internships. Basically anything I could do to break into the industry. I saw all the sights and ventured to all sorts of places in the city. I wasn't there too long when I got homesick, started to run out of money and decided to come home. The day I bought my plane ticket I got a call for an interview with a big public relations firm, but my mind was already set on going back to California, so I declined. I still wonder how my life would have been different if I would have taken that interview.

I came home in July and moved back in with my parents. Boy, was that eye opening! After living in Chico for several years with awesome roommates, I was not ready to be under their roof again. I was also disappointed I hadn't found a job in Los Angeles yet, and that things didn't pan out in New York City when I was there. I had to remind myself that we graduated in the middle of an economic downturn and I know all of my friends had problems finding employment too, with several of them moving back home. I kept telling my Mom I would be stuck in Durham forever. She told me that it wouldn't be that way and I would find something, I just had to have faith.

I had applied for a few jobs in Sacramento, but I really didn't want to live there. It seemed too close to home for my liking. As the capitol of California, Sacramento was known for its politics and I really didn't want to be in the middle of it. But I figured it was better than being stuck in Durham, and I could always look for a job in Los Angeles later.

I ended up applying for a marketing job with a local company and was offered an interview. The day I went to Sacramento for my interview, I also stopped by the public relations and advertising agency where I had done my internship the summer before. When I was there, the head of Client Services at the time passed me in the hall and asked me to stop by his office.

"Hey John!" I said as I walked in.

"How are you?" he asked. "What are you doing in town?"

"I had an interview this morning," I responded.

"Oh," John said surprised. "How did it go?"

"It seems promising, but I'll know more this week. We will see!" I said optimistically. "What did you want to chat about?"

"Well, first of all, I'm sorry you didn't get the position you interviewed for here." I had done a phone interview for an advertising position there, but I knew they were looking for someone bilingual, which I am not, so I wasn't upset about it.

"Oh, no worries! I'm sure the other person is a perfect fit," I responded with a smile.

"Well, we are thinking that we would like to create an account assistant position for you on a few other accounts. Would you be interested in that?" he asked with a smile.

"What?" I said as my mouth gaped open. "Really?"

"Well yeah," John said, smiling again. "We all knew you were a great intern, and we'd like to have you on our team. That is if you want to come back here."

I smiled, pausing at the thought of it. He spoke up again. "Definitely think about it. I know you just had an interview, so don't make a decision right now, but know that we'd like you to be here with us."

I was shocked and flattered. They wanted to create a position for me? The small town intern who spent the summer hocking press releases and putting on press conferences?

"I'm so flattered, John, really," I beamed. "I do want to wait and see what the other company has to say this week, so can I have until Friday to give you an answer?"

"Of course," he replied in his usual calm voice. "We don't even have details on the position, pay, who would be your supervisor, etc.

But we need some help on a few accounts and I knew I wanted to mention it to you before you left."

"Wow. Thank you so much!" I stood to leave his office. "Should I be in touch with you when I hear back about my interview?"

"Yes, just email me and let me know your plan at the end of this week."

"I will do that! Thank you, John. This means a lot." I smiled and turned to leave his office. As I walked down the long hallway, lined with glass window offices I couldn't wipe the smile from my face. They wanted me. They wanted me to be on their team. What a cool thing!

I got in my car and called my Mom.

"You won't believe what happened!" I yelled into the phone.

"What? Are you OK?" she said, worried.

"Yes, yes I'm fine! John just offered me a job!" I shrieked.

"Oh, honey!" Mom said, her smile beaming through the earpiece on my phone. "That is wonderful!"

"Well, he didn't totally offer it to me yet, but I'll tell you more when I get home. I just couldn't wait to share!" I said.

"That's so great! Drive safe and we will see you soon!" she said.

I hung up the phone and drove out of the parking garage on my way back to Durham. I was just offered a job without even interviewing. What was happening? *Maybe Sacramento wouldn't be so bad,* I thought.

Even with the good news, I didn't want to get too excited.

*You've been waiting to work in sports or music for a long time, Laura. Don't give that up yet!* I told myself. *Just wait until you hear back, then make a decision.*

The rest of the week moved at a snail's pace. I figured I should be hearing back about my interview soon. If they didn't call, I'd call them myself and see what the status was. That Friday I still hadn't heard anything, so I placed a call to the manager. She answered and told me they hadn't been able to meet and discuss all the candidates, but they would get back to me the next week.

I thought long and hard about whether or not I felt that waiting would be a good idea, especially when there was a job waiting on the table for me at a place I loved to work.

*Why are you waiting?* I asked myself. *You really want to work there. You know you do.*

In that moment, I made my decision. I emailed John right away and asked him if the offer still stood for the account assistant position. He responded quickly asking me if I was in. I wrote back and let him know I had decided not to move forward with the other company and wanted to come back and work with them. John seemed delighted in his message back and told me he would call with more details later that day.

Next, I emailed the other company to let them know I had accepted another position in Sacramento. Later that day, John called and told me my salary and benefits, and that I would be working under Natalie on several accounts. I was stoked! I couldn't believe I had a job lined up – and that I was moving to Sacramento! I was set to start the position two Mondays later since I needed to find housing and move.

I told my Mom I had accepted the position and she was elated. We made plans to go down to Sacramento with my cousin Megan to look at apartments the next day. While I was really excited to find a job, I still wasn't crazy about moving to Sacramento and I made sure my Mom knew it. I told her I didn't even want to know where the grocery store was because I wouldn't be staying there long anyway. She convinced me that I should know where it was if I didn't want to starve. Moms… they always know what to say to get us to do the right thing.

We drove down on Saturday to see apartments and by the end of the day I had put down a deposit on a spacious one-bedroom apartment in the Natomas area of north Sacramento. It was a gated community, which was appealing for safety since I was a single gal living alone. The unit was on the second floor, also appealing for safety, and my balcony didn't face another building but instead looked over a wide-open field. I was all in on that. The unit was available now so we made plans to move me down the next weekend. Everything was happening so fast, but I was thrilled to be moving out of my parents and into a place of my own.

I had never lived alone, but was excited to see what that was like. Plus, my friend Melissa (and my soon-to-be co-worker) lived in the same complex, so I was happy that I knew someone nearby. I spent the next week packing and shopping for essentials.

The following weekend we drove down to Sacramento with all my belongings in our cow trailer. Man, that was a sight when we pulled into the apartment complex and started unloading. We must have looked like the Beverly Hillbillies! I'm sure my neighbors were stoked.

It took all day to unload my belongings. We had gotten pizza for lunch and had everything moved in by 4pm that afternoon. Mom, my aunt and I took a few trips to the Target for necessities, while my Dad, brother and a couple friends unloaded the big furniture. We all went out for dinner after they were done, and then my family headed home.

When they left, I walked back upstairs and stood in my quiet apartment.

*This place is mine*, I thought. I walked over, plopped down on my new couch and put my feet up on the coffee table.

I looked around and said out loud, "I could get used to this!"

I spent the next day unpacking, and I was able to get my closet put together and finish putting away all of my kitchen items. That's when I decided to make my first trip to the grocery store. There was a Raley's right up the street so I headed over, picked up groceries and headed back home to make some dinner. My apartment was starting to feel like home.

On Monday I got up early to get ready for work. I wanted to give myself plenty of time to get to the office. I had already picked out a power outfit for my first day so after I showered and ate breakfast, I got dressed and left for work.

I found that my trip to work would take about 30 minutes with traffic, but still arrived early. When I walked into the office, it felt like home. Probably because I had just interned there a year before.

*Don't get too comfortable, Laura. You will be leaving here soon enough*. I said to myself. I still dreamt of moving to Los Angeles to work in the music industry. *This job is just a stepping stone to bigger and better things.*

I met with our human resources manager to fill out all my paperwork and she showed me to my desk. After I got settled, I sat down with my new supervisor, Natalie, to discuss my role. We had a great chat then went out to lunch with a few of our other team members and friends. Things were getting off to a good start and I was feeling OK about the move to Sacramento, at least for the time being.

I called my Mom on my way home from work that day and told her I had a great first day. I also told her I still planned to move to Los Angeles after working there for a while. What was "a while"? Well, I didn't know at that point, but I thought maybe a year.

Being back at the agency felt good and comfortable for me from the start. I really enjoyed my co-workers, and the work we did at the agency was stellar. I felt like I had found a good place to start my career. I also knew so much about the agency already that falling into the position was an easy transition.

I made a ton of friends as I got to know people in the industry too. My co-workers and I went out for drinks after work and hung out on the weekends. Melissa and I hung out often too. I was starting to find my groove the longer I was in Sacramento.

The Sacramento Kings basketball season had started and our company president had season tickets. I was very lucky to be invited to some games and had such a blast. I was becoming a Kings fan. I actually liked Sacramento! I was making friends. I was finding my groove. Who was I?

I was becoming a Sacramentan. And that was weird. I knew where all my favorite restaurants were. I knew the ins and outs of parking downtown. I had developed friendships I never thought I would, and over the next few months I couldn't imagine moving away from Sacramento. It was just close enough to my family, and just far enough away from them at the same time. It was close to San Francisco and the beach, and just as close to the mountains and Lake Tahoe. What was there not to like about Sacramento?

I spent the next few years really making Sacramento a home. I moved several times into different apartments, condos, houses and in June 2008 right before I started training for my first marathon, I purchased a condo that would be my home for eight years. I had made Sacramento a home even though I swore I would never stay there.

In the years following, I developed my running career and made a whole new set of friends that are now my best friends. I never thought that's where I would end up. I was SURE I would be moving away before I could blink. But even though I thought Sacramento wasn't the place for me, I found that it really was. It was a big city, but not Los Angeles. It was full of great places to go and fun things to do. I had made Sacramento my home and loved it.

◆ ◆ ◆

My mom had told me to just try out Sacramento and see if I could make it work. She had faith in me to give myself a chance to love something that I was determined NOT to love. She knew that I would at least learn more about myself there, than I would if I kept trying to wait to move to Los Angeles.

Living in a city I thought I would hate (or wanted to hate), taught me a lot about how we try to plan out and control our lives. You think you absolutely won't do certain things and you absolutely will do others. You have a plan in your head and tell people they are crazy when they put another idea in front of you. But really, you have to believe that there is a plan for where you will end up. Because in the end, you will end up right where you were meant to be. Whether it's in your personal life, professional life, or anything else, there is a reason you end up where you are.

I wouldn't change a thing about starting my career and life in Sacramento. This area has become my home and it introduced me to running, which has become my life passion. Sacramento is a great place to live. It's a wonderful city and I will love it forever.

# FIFTEEN
## Sunday, June 28, 2015 – Mile 78 - 4:19 a.m.

"Gosh, this is cold!" I laughed as we made our way through the shallow entry to the Rucky Chucky river crossing. The safety cable stretched across the river on our left as we tried to maintain our balance on the slippery rocks.

"Hold onto the cable at all times with at least one hand," a volunteer ordered.

"You got it!" I replied. "I'm not going swimming in this!"

Brad led the way across the river, showing me the best places to put my feet as the water got deeper. Within no time, the water was up to our knees. The cable was lined with volunteers wearing wetsuits standing in water up to their waists. They held the line steady as we crossed. There were glow sticks dropped in the water so we could see how deep it was with each step.

"There's a large rock right here where my leg is," one volunteer said to me as I passed her. "It's slippery so be careful and hold on,"

"Thank you!" I said cheerily. "And thank you for being out here!"

"You're welcome!" she replied. "You're doing great."

My next step took me much deeper into the water, covering my running shorts. "Woooo! That's chilly!"

"Just keep moving," Brad said. "We're about halfway across."

"Bob, I'm coming!" I yelled out, sounding a bit crazy.

"I hear you!" he yelled back.

Brad and I continued to make our way across the cold water, over large boulders and slimy rocks. We neared the other side where there were lights up in the trees and a photographer waited by the waters edge taking our picture.

Then I saw Bob on the dry rocks near the water exit.

"Bob! I feel GREAT!" I yelled. At this point in the race I was quite delirious. Bob said that my eyes were open so wide that I looked as if I might be afraid to relax them for fear that they may shut tightly, and permanently. And I was yelling a lot, like I didn't know how to control the volume of my voice.

"I have a drop bag," I said to Bob and he headed over to grab it. He pulled out the towel I had inside so I could dry off a bit before we climbed up the hill. He also handed me a Pepsi from inside that I passed off to Brad, as I wasn't wanting anything.

I dried my legs and wrapped the towel around me. I wasn't very cold but I felt like I needed to have it around me for some reason.

"Let's go," Bob said.

We began the 2-mile trek up to the Green Gate aid station right away. I knew there was no time to waste in getting up and over the mountain to the more runnable section on the other side.

"What time is it?" I asked Brad.

"4:25 a.m," Brad replied. "We're ahead of the cutoff by more than 30 minutes now. Great job!" He also knew at that time that we were finally back to even with the 30-hour pace. That was Brad and Bob's goal for the climb to Green Gate, to get me back even with the 30-hour pace so I could make up time and not be down to the wire at the finish.

"Oh, thank goodness," I replied, relieved. "Where's my crew?"

"They are on their way," Bob replied. Just then they appeared, walking down the hill towards us.

"Hi," I said calmly. All of a sudden exhaustion started to come over me. My crew was there and Bob was there so my mind started to relax. Running this distance can have varying effects on people. It's not uncommon to become cranky or irritated, not only from the distance, but from sleep deprivation as well.

Joe came up next to me, looking visibly concerned for my condition. I was still wide eyed, but quiet and tired at the same time. Bob reached over and grabbed the towel that was now getting in the way of my walking and carried it the rest of the way up the hill.

"You're doing great," Carol said. "Do you want me to carry anything for you?"

"Fuck off, Carol," I replied. She immediately got quiet. I was frustrated, tired and lashed out at my crew. It wasn't one of my best moments, that's for sure. I had been awake for 24 hours. I was ahead of the cutoffs but just barely – even with the 30-hour time. And I was depleted from exerting myself so much over 78 miles.

We continued up the hill, with my crew and Brad chatting about everything that had happened so far. Bob sat back and absorbed all the information from my team to be well versed on our plans moving forward. I trudged along in my own silent state.

"She's been following her fueling plan and eating about every 40 minutes. She's eating soup and drinking Coke in the aid stations," he continued, looking at Bob as if to ask him to make mental notes. "She's drinking her fluids but you have to remind her since it's not super warm right now. She's been refilling one bottle of fluid at almost every aid station."

"Any complaints over pain, chafing, etc.?" Carol asked.

"She keeps saying her shins hurt and talked about putting Tiger Balm on them at Green Gate. Do you have Tiger Balm?"

"Yes, it's up top where we are set up," she said.

"Great," he said. "She also told me she took some Tylenol at El Dorado Creek so she could take more of that now if you have it."

"I'll pull that out too. Thanks," Carol responded.

"I'm tired, guys," I said to everyone.

"We know," Brad replied. "At the aid station you can rest for a moment before Bob takes you out."

"Oh good," I said, sighing. I needed a break bad.

We power-hiked the remainder of the two miles to the Green Gate aid station. The dust kicked up by all the runners hung in the air and glowed in the light from our headlamps. The darkness of the early morning was quiet. There were other runners moving behind and in front of me. They had crews and pacers accompanying them as well.

We passed a few groups of crews and pacers that were heading down to meet their runners as they came across the river. "Great job runner!" they offered as they allowed us to pass by on the wide dirt road.

The trail was clear of trees, which allowed for a great view of the sky. The moon was brilliant, lighting up the trail for us, along with our head-lamps. The calm, serene feeling of the last few moments hiking up was just the restoration I needed going into the final 20 miles of the race.

"We're set up right over here," Carol directed as we made our way to the black and white cow blanket.

"Do we have Tiger Balm?" I asked.

"Yes," she replied. "Take a seat and I'll put it on you."

"Give me your bottles," Joe said and I handed them over.

I carefully sat down on the blanket as Carol knelt in front of me and pulled out the small glass jar of Tiger Balm. I tossed my knuckle light onto the blanket and rolled my leg sleeves up a few inches so she could apply the balm to the sore parts. Despite snapping at Carol earlier, she had taken my exhaustion in stride, knowing that I wasn't exactly myself during all of this.

Just then an aid station volunteer appeared and squatted down next to me.

"Hey Laura! You look amazing! What can I get you?" she asked.

"I'd love to take some pretzels with me," I said.

"I'll get you a baggie, hang on." She ran off towards the food tables.

"I just need Tiger Balm here on my shins," I said to Carol. "They've been killing me since I was walking near Last Chance. I know I over did it like I did at Javelina, but oh well!"

Carol rubbed the Tiger Balm into my shins and pulled my calf sleeves back down. "OK, let's get you up. I don't want you sitting for long."

As she helped me up, the aid station volunteer appeared again with a baggie of pretzels. She handed them to me and said, "You're doing great. Keep it up."

"Thank you so much," I replied.

Joe handed me my handheld bottles he had refilled with Skratch.

"Thank you honey," I said to Joe as Bob took the baggie of pretzels from me and tucked it in his pocket to eat later.

"Here, take these," Carol said as she handed me two Tylenol. I drank them down with a swig of Skratch.

"What time is it?" I asked.

"5 a.m.," Bob replied. "Let's go."

I had now been running for a full 24 hours. I kissed Joe and thanked my crew. Bob and I walked out of the aid station towards the trail entrance just up the road.

"You can do this Laura. This is your chance to relax and stop thinking. Just try to do what I tell you and stay upright." Bob was speaking seriously, but still kind as we reached the gate to the trail. "Trust me to keep us ahead of the cutoffs. You just pay attention to your running and the trail. Hydrate, eat and keep moving. Leave the rest to me. Got it?"

"I got it Bob," I replied. I felt excited to have Bob with me. Brad had been an excellent and very efficient pacer, but seeing a new face was always nice. Plus, I knew the sun was coming up soon which gave me hope as we made our way down the trail.

"Are we going to make it?" I quietly asked Bob.

"We're going to make it, but you have to push harder than you've ever pushed before. OK?"

"Yes. I'll do whatever it takes."

"Let's move," Bob said. "Look, the sun is coming up."

I glanced up ahead and between the trees I could see the sky was lightening. "Just get to the sunshine, right Bob?"

"You made it to the sunshine, Laura." Although I couldn't see his face, I could tell he was smiling when he said it.

We began trotting down the trail. I could barely see the light from my headlamp anymore, but I left it on as the shadows from the trees overhead made it difficult to see at times. Soon we made a right-hand turn onto a single-track trail. We cruised along with the sunlight becoming brighter each step.

We had made it to the sunshine. If you are going to take more than 24 hours to run a 100-mile race, reaching the sunshine on the next day is the best feeling. It's like everything from the previous 24 hours goes away. I had the same feeling when I ran my first 100 in Arizona. The sun coming up over the mountains in the desert was brilliant, making me feel like I had just woken up from a long night sleep, except I hadn't slept at all. Coming into the daylight of the canyon was the same feeling of elation and excitement. While we still couldn't see the actual sun, we had made it to the sunshine.

Soon we reached a portion of the trail I knew from running the Way Too Cool 50k several times. Two trails merged, and we encountered a runner who had made a wrong turn and was worried about finishing.

"You will be fine, just tuck in behind us and we will bring you through this part of the course," Bob said to the runner. "You will get there." He stayed with us for a bit, but we eventually lost him as we neared the Auburn Lake Trails (ALT) aid station.

We cruised down the single-track switchbacks into the clearing and headed down the gravel road towards the aid station area. That's when we saw our co-worker Lisa and her husband Scott. They lived just up the road in Auburn Lake Trails and had come down to the aid station to cheer us on.

"Hey guys!" I yelled as we ran by towards the aid station. Lisa started snapping photos as we ran by her and Scott. They followed us along the big loop to the food tables and continued taking pictures.

When we arrived at the food tables, Bob grabbed a cup of soup and immediately handed it to me as I held my handhelds in one hand.

A medic came up beside me looking a bit concerned. "How are you feeling?"

I glimpsed at Bob shakily, "I'm good." My eyes were still wide open, and I was listening to Bob's every word as I sipped my soup.

"You sure?" the medic said.

"Yup," I replied. "I'm peeing as needed and I just went number two at Rucky Chucky. I'm eating and I feel good." (too much information, I know… but these are the things they're concerned about when you're running 100 miles.)

"OK," she said, looking over at Bob. The medic seemed a bit worried and I'm sure she was with all the runners who came through this aid station. I had just run more than 85 miles and was pretty loopy, but I felt good all things considered.

"She's good. I got her. Don't worry," Bob replied firmly.

I know Bob was using his eyes to tell them not to mess with his runner in the politest way he could. He could be defensive like that. Bob took pacing very seriously, and he wasn't going to let anything get in the way of our finish.

"I'm just tired. Shouldn't I be tired right now though?" I asked as I peered at Bob again.

"You're doing great. Drink and let's move," he instructed.

I downed the soup and threw away the cup in the trash can. "Lisa, Scott, thank you for coming down!" I said as we headed towards the exit of the aid station.

"Let's go!" Bob said, with excitement. I knew he was concerned about the clock, but I trusted he knew exactly what we needed to do to get to the finish in time.

We made our way down the trail across the first small creek crossing. As we came to the next crossing, we slowed and walked carefully over the rocks. We stepped out on the dirt path and again I asked Bob, "Are we going to make it?"

"Of course we are going to make it," he replied confidently. "Leave the hard thinking to me. You just run."

"You got it, Bob," I said. "I'll do whatever it takes." He began to run and I trotted behind him following his feet along the worn dirt path. "Bob, I don't care how much this hurts. It will hurt so much more to tell people I didn't get a buckle." I could feel the tears start to sting my eyes.

The lack of sleep was starting to wear on me even more. I blinked back the tears, inhaled a deep breath and charged on as we took the rolling single track at a quicker pace.

"How far are we from Brown's Bar?" I asked.

"About four miles. We will be there in no time," Bob stated, all business in this moment. "Just keep plugging along." He pulled the pace chart from his pocket and glanced at his watch.

"We're just fine," he said again. Then he picked up the pace and I could tell we needed to move faster to make up more time.

"What time did we come into ALT?" I asked.

"You clocked at 6:29 a.m.," he replied.

I was finally ahead of the 30-hour time. By only one minute, but I was ahead of the time, at the very least. I had gotten to even with the time at mile 80, but I felt even better knowing that now I was actually ahead of it and now we just had to tick off more of a cushion for ourselves.

Bob and I followed the rolling single track for the next few miles. I hadn't trained this portion of the trail a lot because I had run it so many times in previous years training for the Way Too Cool 50K. It had become pretty engrained in my brain, so I knew most of it by heart. The sun had risen by now, though the trail remained shaded, as it was on the north side of the mountain. It was starting to get warm, but not too bad compared to the heat of the day before. I had another Clif gel and was feeling pretty good as we ran along. I was sleepy, but did feel another burst of energy with the new day and sunshine.

We snaked along the edge of the canyon and finally started to hear the music from the Brown's Bar aid station at mile 90.

"We're almost there Bob!" I yelled. I was elated at the possibility of only being 10 miles out from the finish.

"We are," he said. "Stay focused. Let's get in and get out. Grab what you need and move, OK?"

"Yup," I replied.

As we came into the aid station, I went straight for the food table to have a volunteer fill my water bottle. I handed off one bottle, tucking the other under my arm, and grabbed a cup of soup and some Coke. You'd think that I'd be tired of the same thing over and over, but in an ultra you go with what works. And you try something new when it doesn't work anymore. Since soup and Coke were working, I stuck to it.

"Hey there," one volunteer said. "You better hurry, you're right on the cutoffs."

"She's fine!" Bob said in a stern, do-not-say-anything-to-my-runner voice. I could tell he was mad at the guy for saying anything to me about a cutoff.

I examined Bob with big eyes. I'm sure he could see the alarm on my face as I wondered if we would make it.

"You're fine," Bob said to reassure me. He put a hand on my shoulder and guided me towards the exit of the aid station. He went back to get my bottle from the volunteer as I drank the rest of my soup and Coke.

"You ready?" he asked, handing me my bottle as I threw away my cups.

"Yeah," I said, shakily. "What time is it?"

"7:35," he replied. "Don't think about the time."

"Are we gonna make it, Bob?" I asked for what must have seemed like the millionth time.

"We are going to make it," he said. "I can't believe that guy said that. We are fine. Let's go!"

We set off down Brown's Ravine towards the first short creek crossing. I could see Bob pull the pace chart out of his pocket again to check our time. He seemed a bit unnerved, but kept his cool in order to keep me calm. Or so I thought. Bob knew all along that I was now 15 minutes ahead of the 30-hour time. But he wasn't about to tell me.

"Take it easy on the downhills. Really watch your footing," Bob instructed.

This section of the course had lots of rocks and ruts in the trail. Along with berry vines that snaked out onto the path in places, just waiting to get tripped up on your shoes. Of course, it had to be like this on the last stretch of this race.

We reached the bottom of Brown's Bar and made the left onto Quarry Road. "We're on Quarry!" I said to Bob excitedly.

"We are!" he replied. "We're going to run this, OK?"

"Even the hills?" I asked.

"Even the hills. I'll let you walk the big ones but this is where we can make up some more time. OK?"

"OK. I'll do whatever you say to get to that buckle," I replied wearily. I trusted Bob, but fatigue was really starting to set in and my mental toughness was truly wavering. I didn't know what would happen anymore. My brain couldn't calculate minutes so I just kept putting one foot in front of the other.

We ran along quickly, taking advantage of the easy rolling road. Quarry was a wide road with plenty of space to run. It was well-maintained with dirt and gravel and free of any big dangers. While I didn't want to run the whole thing, I would certainly do whatever Bob told me at this point.

We came to the left turn leading up to the Highway 49 aid station as Bob said, "OK, you did great running on Quarry. Now let's take on this climb. Power up, OK?"

"OK," I replied, out of breath.

We began hiking up the steep climb of single track. The trail was very narrow and covered in ruts, holes and rocks. We had to keep our pace up, all the while being careful with each step along the way.

Bob noticed I was slowing and offered some encouragement. "Laura, now's the time to get mad and leave it out here," he shouted back at me. "Just get really damn mad! Show the trail who is boss!"

I slowed and stopped, bent over with my hands on my knees and started crying.

"Bob! I'm trying so hard! I'm doing the best I can!" I said in between sobs.

Bob immediately went into repair mode. "Oh!" he said as he turned around to face me. He knew he had crossed an emotional line and had to repair it fast to keep me moving. "You're doing so great out here! I was just trying to encourage you. Let's move. Just keep walking the way you were. You're doing amazing!"

"OK," I choked out. "I'm sorry, Bob. I'm trying, really I am."

"Oh, I know you are!" he said. "I'm just getting excited is all!" He had finished this race himself so he knew how thrilling it was to be less than 10 miles from the finish line.

We marched up the trail and through the tiny creek crossings until we reached the gravel road leading us to the next single track. We made our way through another water crossing and started taking on the rolling hills.

That's when I heard it. Highway 49. Not the aid station, but the highway – and the cars on it. I knew where I was. I knew we were very close to the road crossing at the Highway 49 aid station.

"I know all of this," I said to myself. "I know where I am and what I have to do."

Bob picked up the pace, and I obediently followed. We were now running my road pace as we bounded along the hills towards the road.

As we neared the aid station Bob giddily said, "Do you hear it? They are going to announce your name as you cross the road! And your crew will be there!"

"Let's go!" I replied.

We trotted down the trail and through the trees I could see the aid station to our right. There were lights still hanging, tents, decorations, volunteers and tons of crew members standing around waiting for their runners.

We cruised down the hill turning right past the course monitor who radioed in my bib number. The trail changed from dirt to gravel as we approached the highway crossing. The ground finally felt light under my feet, because I knew we were almost home. I knew we had made it to a pivotal point in the race. We were now seven miles from the finish. Seven miles.

Then we heard it. "Here's bib number 1-2-6, Laura Langerwerf! Yay, Laura!" the announcer yelled as I ran across the road into the aid station.

# SIXTEEN
## November 2014

"I just don't know how I can do this!" I cried as I talked to my Mom on speakerphone. I was in my car on the way to work and stressing out about my finances. Bills were due and while I had the money, I felt like I barely had enough to eat once everything was paid.

Rewind back to my 2002-2003 school year in college. When I was at Chico State, I lived away from home for two years. (My hometown was a 20-minute drive from school, but I wanted to live in Chico anyway.) I had financial aid, as well as a loan for the last two years of school so that I could live on my own. Each semester when I got my financial aid and loan money, I took the cash I allotted for rent and bills and put it in monthly envelopes in my parents' safe so I wouldn't be tempted to spend it. I was very smart with my money in that aspect. Then I got my first credit card – and it all went downhill from there.

When I graduated and moved to Sacramento for my first job, I rented a nice apartment within my means. Like I did in college, I made sure I set aside money for bills every month so I wouldn't be broke when they arrived in my mailbox. However, I had credit cards. A few of them. And when there were things I wanted to purchase but I didn't have the budget, I used the cards. Naively, I saw my lines of credit as my money to spend and just pay off as I went.

I charged vacations and furniture, along with nights out on the town and gifts. Most of the time I paid it off each month, but sometimes I would have a higher purchase and wouldn't be able to afford paying the whole balance off, so I'd pay more than the minimum and just let the balance sit there.

Mind you, at this point I made plenty of money to live a comfortable life. I could afford my bills and I could buy plenty of groceries at the local Raley's. I could eat out with friends if I wanted to. I just didn't have a real awareness of my credit card debt and how it was affecting my life.

Fast forward to four years later: Summer 2008. I was still at my first public relations and advertising job and I was making a great salary. After conversations with my parents, I decided to purchase a new condo in North Sacramento so I wouldn't be "throwing away money on rent," at least that's what I told myself. I knew how much I could afford, and my parents offered to cover my gas bills so I'd have a little extra cushion in my budget too.

In no time I was living in a swanky, brand new, three-bedroom, 2.5 bath condo. I could afford it (barely), but I felt like that was exactly what I should be doing. I had always known what debt was and that if you pinched every penny out of your budget and could still make ends meet, you would be fine.

In 2010, I left my first job to go to a different firm and received a solid raise. Wow! I have more money now! What else can I spend it on? I don't think I consciously thought that, but when I saw more dollars on my paycheck, my first inclination wasn't to pay off my debt. It was to spend! So what did I do? I bought a new car! Well, a used car – but new to me. Heck, I could afford it so why not?

Let's be honest – I've always been a natural spender. When I was little, I would do odd jobs around the farm to make a few dollars here or there. Then I would hop on my bike or get a ride to Durham (about three miles up the road) to buy some penny candy at a local shop, Jerry's Clothes and Things. Having money burned a hole in my pocket. I wanted to spend, spend, spend everything I earned.

I had barely put away anything for retirement by that point because I didn't want to sacrifice my hard earned money on that old-age nonsense. I would figure out retirement when it was time to retire!

I worked at my second advertising job for two years before I was unfortunately laid off (look back at chapter six for that story) and realized what a hole I was really in.

*Holy crap.* I thought. *I can barely afford my mortgage on unemployment.*

Luckily, I had very supportive parents who continued to pay for my gas and gave me some extra cash each month to help make ends meet. But did I stop spending like I was before? Nope. Why did they keep giving me money? Probably because they are the most giving and loving parents, and they only want their kids to have everything they've dreamed of.

My parents have always worked extremely hard. They had a dairy farm for many years and now raise beef cattle and farm walnuts. Growing up I knew that we were in debt (dairy farm life for a small farmer is not lucrative), but I didn't really understand what that meant. In the end, no matter the debt, they still put food on the table and clothes on our backs, so we knew we were OK. When I found myself in debt, I figured it was OK and I would find a way out of it, or maybe my parents would help, since they had always helped me out before.

So when I lost my job in January 2013 and kept spending the way I was before, I found myself going even further into debt. I ended up using another credit card my bank had given me just to have a cushion because as you know by now, I did not have any sort of backup plan or emergency fund to speak of. I found another job in April 2013 that paid more than my measly unemployment, but at that time I was also going into debt with massage school loans. I was in a hole that I really didn't know how to get out of.

When I became a certified massage therapist in October 2013 (in California this can happen once you've been in school for 500 hours – our school had a more than 1,000 hour program so we were certified to begin working mid-schooling), I started working on clients right away. Being a runner, I had developed quite a network of friends who also became clients of mine. I would have them either come to my home (I had a guest room in my home that became my massage therapy room) or I would take my table to their place for appointments. After awhile, I needed more help with rent (beyond my current roommate), so I rented out the second room and became a traveling massage therapist only.

I was able to work 40 hours a week at my job and go to school 20 hours a week while finishing my massage therapy degree, all while working on 3-4 clients a week to provide a little extra income. Along with this, I was running ultra-marathons that left me with pretty much no other time in my schedule for anything but running. I was working myself to the bone. And I was still in debt.

I finished massage therapy school in September 2014, a few months before I was set to run my first 100-mile race in Arizona. I started to take on more clients so I could afford to pay for my crew and I to fly to Arizona and do all the necessary race things. This was also when the student loans started to set in, so I had a whole new set of problems to deal with.

◆ ◆ ◆

I'll be completely transparent about the real hole I was in. I had $52,000 in debt that broke down like this:
- $3,000 – dental bills
- $8,000 – car debt
- $12,000 – credit cards
- $29,000 – massage school loans

I also owned a condo that was barely in the positive. I owed $185,000 on my loan. I had purchased it at the height of the market for $272,000 and it was now only worth about $215,000, providing little equity.

I met Joe in November 2014 when I was drowning in debt and working a ton, but I still had no idea how to get out of this mess. I didn't understand how to pay it off or fix the situation I had gotten myself into. Which brings me back to the beginning of this chapter. I was crying on the phone to my Mom on the way to work. This was not something foreign to me as at the time she was the person I vented to when the sky was falling. And it certainly felt like the sky was falling in those stressful years.

When I met Joe, the tables turned. He had spent years of his life living on two credit cards. American Express and Discover. He would put everything on them each month and pay them off at the end of the month. He earned oodles of points, but never went into "debt". He also had a home and a strong 401K he had been saving in since he started working in his early 20s. I saw him as a guy who had it all together. He knew what he was doing, and he was on top of his life financially.

Then came our big fight. You can refer back to chapter 8 for the nitty-gritty of that fight/break-up/make-up, but let's just say it wasn't pretty. And I was mostly at fault for it. While I had no idea how to get myself out of debt, I also didn't want ANYONE to tell me how to spend my money. Or how to get out of debt. Quite the conundrum, right?

Well, after our fight/break-up/make-up, Joe told me that if we were going to get married someday, we had to be on the same page with our finances. We agreed that we would take Dave Ramsey's class, Financial Peace University, after we got engaged. I decided at that point to start working on my debt so I wouldn't go into a marriage with any debt. I had started listening to Dave Ramsey's podcast, absorbing his teachings and the baby steps.

This was around April 2015. I was in the height of Western States training, still working at Fleet Feet Sacramento and working on massage clients 3-4 evenings of the week after work. Life was nuts, but I knew I needed to get a handle on it so I could make things better. A very smart man, Albert Einstein, once said, "The definition of insanity is doing the same thing over and over again, and expecting a different result."

In late 2014, this was me. This was me in every sense of the word. I kept spending like I had money, when I was completely broke. Like the kind of broke where you go to Starbucks and pray your card goes through. The kind of broke where I was charging the basics – like my groceries – on my credit card. I kept whining to my Mom about how I would never get out of debt, but I was digging myself into a bigger hole because I was doing the same thing over and over again. After I met Joe, my perspective changed and I realized that debt wasn't the problem. It was me.

I had to make a change. Saying that I didn't know how wasn't going to change the end result at all. I had to accept that I was doing things wrong and actively not do those things anymore.

I asked Joe for the amortization spreadsheet he had made. I put all of my debts in it, from smallest to largest, to see how long it would take me to pay them off. It was going to take forever at my current job and activity load. That's when Joe and I sat down to have a conversation, and he said something that made complete sense.

"Laura, I know you love your condo," he said, "But do you want to live there forever?"

"I do love my condo. It's the first home I've owned," I replied. "But no, I don't plan to live there forever."

"Then I think it's time to consider selling it," Joe said flatly.

"What?" I replied, shocked. "Where will I live? That's crazy! It's my home!" I was starting to get upset.

"I know. I know," he replied, laying a hand on my arm. "I would never tell you to sell it and leave you without a place to live."

"Well, what would I do?" I asked, obviously frazzled.

"Come live with me," he said with a smile. "Come move into my apartment. I'm already paying the rent and I don't need help to do that, so you will save money there."

"You want me to sell my condo and move into your 900-square foot, one-bedroom apartment. With my dog?" I asked with a laugh.

"Yes," Joe said with a straight face. "You and Nashville."

I laughed out loud at this point. *What was he thinking? How would we do that?*

"Where would I put all my stuff?" I asked, laughing again.

"Here's the honest truth," he said. "It's stuff. And how much of it do you really, really need?"

That was an eye-opening statement for me. It was just stuff. I had oodles of movies, CDs, books, photographs from high school, trinkets, clothing I never wore, more purses and pairs of shoes than I could ever want, things for my spare bedroom that I didn't need, and seriously, more towels that I knew what to do with. All things that I felt I "needed" to make me whole. In the end, getting rid of the "stuff" and making changes actually didn't seem like a bad idea.

We discussed this plan a bit more before going to my parents with it. They had helped me put the down payment on my condo, so I felt the need to include them in my decision, even though I was going to move forward without their permission. We told them what we were going to do and while they balked at it a bit, as Joe had broken up with me once before, in the end they agreed it would be a good idea.

So we went about cleaning out my condo and preparing it for sale. We took some time to do this and hired my friend Mike to be our realtor for the sale process. Once I had taken loads and loads (and loads) of boxes to Goodwill, I sold all my furniture and kept only the things I really needed and I moved in with Joe. This all happened on Memorial Day Weekend, which also happened to be the weekend of the Western States training runs. Why I chose to do that much in such a crazy time of my life, I will never know. What I do know is that you grow from adversity and I was putting myself in a place to grow a lot.

After I got moved in, my condo went up for sale. We listed it at $215,000 and it stayed on the market for a few weeks before we got into contract. Luckily, it was a cash buyer so the sale was completed in some 20 days or so. I took the $30,000 I had in equity and threw it straight at my debt. I was able to knock out the dental bills, car loan, credit cards and part of my student loans in one fell swoop. I had $22,000 left to pay off. It was June 2015.

I moved forward to focus on running Western States, knowing that I would start really attacking my debt come in July. We visited Yosemite National Park for Joe's birthday. It was our first time there and I had a feeling it would be a special trip for us. On July 18, 2015 we took a hike up to Cloud's Rest, one of the highest points in the park. Joe proposed to me near the top, making me the happiest woman ever. And also making all my debt so much more real. Now I knew I had to get cracking on my debt so I could pay it off before we got married.

I continued working 40 hours a week at my day job and took on even more massage therapy clients. I was seeing 8-10 clients each week in addition to my full-time gig, and put every extra penny I could squeeze out of my budget onto my debt. I only went out to eat one time a month or if Joe was paying. It took me nine months, but on March 18, 2016 I pushed the button to pay off my last student loan. I was officially debt-free!!

Who was this girl and what had happened to make her actually have control of her life? I found a path I could follow that would help me. I also stopped the insanity of doing the same thing over and over and looking for a different result. I chose to do better and to be better. I chose to grow up and become a responsible human being. I chose to live with situations where I had to say no because I didn't have the money.

Joe and I now live a debt-free lifestyle. We do not have credit cards. The only loan we have is for our home – a 15-year mortgage with a payment is no more than 25% of our monthly income. We just bought a car for cash. That's right, CASH. We brought in a cashier's check for most of the amount and wrote a personal check for the rest. Let me tell you… driving away knowing the car was outright ours was an amazing feeling.

What did I learn from being in debt? I learned that you can get into debt easily, but you can't just walk out of it. You can charge all the things you "want" and "need," but you can't get the money back and it will take much longer than you got in, to get out. I also learned that the quote about insanity is true, not only with debt, but with so many other things. If you keep doing the same thing, you won't get any better.

If you keep hanging out with the same people and don't challenge yourself, you won't be any better. If you keep running the same pace, you won't get any stronger. If you choose to hike the hills slowly, you will never learn to hike them with quickness to make them an advantage in a race. The perseverance it took to start my get-out-of-debt journey taught me that I could persevere in 100 miles and conquer it. It taught me that I had to go outside of my comfort zone, or I would never learn to be better than I already was. It taught me that in order to improve, I had to be uncomfortable.

Step outside of yourself and be better. Challenge yourself to do more. Don't rely on the "Oh, that's just the way I am" excuse, because that's just what it is, an excuse. A hundred miles is no joke, but more than that, 100 miles is something you have to choose to conquer. It won't just happen.

211

# SEVENTEEN
## Sunday, June 28, 2015 – Mile 93 - 8:33 a.m.

"Do I smell bacon?" The aroma hit me fast as I ran across the road into the Highway 49 aid station.

"You do!" Bob said, "I'll try to get you some. Joe is right over there," he said pointing in the direction of my crew as he headed towards the aid station tables.

Two volunteers came up to me to ask what I needed. I handed one of them a bottle and asked him to fill it with water and Skratch powder. Then Joe walked up to me and I told him I had already given my bottle to one of the aid station volunteers.

"Where's Carol?" I asked and saw her over Joe's shoulder. I stepped around him to move towards her and hand off the extra bottle.

"I got you," Carol said as I walked toward her handing her my bottle.

"I don't need the extra gel or belt I had planned on," I told her as I pulled off the long sleeve tied around my neck.

I turned and saw Andy, his wife Sarah and their kids, Matt, Joe and Gianna, standing there. "Hi guys! Thank you for coming out!"

"Hi!" they all said, staring up at me with wide eyes. The kids were only 10-12 years old then. I'm sure I looked really crazy since they hadn't seen me in a while. It had been several months of training and work since I had seen them – and I was in much worse shape now.

I handed Carol my long sleeve and looked at Sarah. "Thank you for coming out and bringing these guys!"

"We wouldn't miss this!" Sarah replied. "We will be at the finish too."

"Awesome!" I said. "Be sure to come to Robie point to run in with me."

Carol had already gotten my Fleet Feet Sacramento Racing tank ready as she took my long sleeve, pack and one of my bottles.

Bob handed me some soup. "Drink this," he instructed as he headed back to the table to get me some Coke.

Carol grabbed my head-lamp off my head, tucking it in her bag. "Give me your food," she said, taking the soup. "Turn your hat around and fix your ponytail." I did as I was instructed. She held up my orange Fleet Feet Sacramento Racing tank top.

"You wanted to put this on here instead of Robie. Do you still want to do that?"

"Yes," I replied as I pulled my yellow tank top off and shimmied into the orange one. I'm sure I scared Andy's kids by standing there in my sports bra. Honestly, modesty really goes out the window at hour 27 of a race.

I grabbed my soup from Carol and started drinking it. Bob came up and handed me some soda, then headed back to the table to see if there was anything else I needed.

"I'm so glad to see you all!" I said to my crew. "Thank you so much."

Bob came back, hovering nervously as I stood talking to everyone. Joe handed Bob my bottle and kissed me goodbye. I downed the Coke and looked at Bob. "Let's go," he instructed, putting his hand on my back leading me towards the exit of the aid station while I sipped the soup.

I started heading for the food table and a woman volunteer stopped me. "You need to drink that soup and get out of here or I'm going to take it from you."

Bob looked impatient, so I turned and walked towards the exit with the volunteer following me as I still sipped my soup.

"Throw it away here," she said with a smile. "Get out of here! You've got a race to run!" she yelled, kind of giggling at how out of it I was. I'm sure Bob was thrilled when she did that.

I turned and yelled back a loud "Thank you all!" to my crew and the volunteers.

I was so delirious I barely knew what I was doing anymore. Bob ushered me out of the aid station while I was still trying to turn back and chat with more of the volunteers.

"Let's move!" Bob handed me my handheld and led me up the long hill towards the meadow. We ran part of the uphill and walked the steeper, rocky sections as we made our way through the single track. We reached the top and then started across the meadow. That's when I knew things were looking up.

I felt great in a clean shirt. My body felt fueled. And I knew the downhill we called "Rollercoaster" was coming up next. It was easily one of my favorite places to run. The single-track trail was downhill for a mile or so. The terrain was easy to run, shaded and a good decline so you could cruise down not too fast and not too slow. When you took this section at a nice pace, gravity would push you right along, you just had to move your feet. It felt like a rollercoaster ride as you flew down it. And today, I was excited to take it quick.

We crossed through the sunny, dry grass of the meadow and made the sweeping right onto the downhill single track. Then my right ankle started to hurt.

*What is that?* I thought. *This is not happening!* I continued down the hill, allowing my feet to pitter-patter lightly down the trail, enjoying the speed of Rollercoaster.

"Bob," I said. "My ankle really hurts."

"Everything may hurt at this point, Laura," Bob replied matter-of-factly. "Just keep moving down the hill."

I kept trotting downhill, following Bob's feet and eventually the pain subsided and I felt good again. "I've got this," I said to myself.

"What time did we come through Highway 49?" I asked Bob.

"Right around 8:30," he replied. That put us 30 minutes ahead of the 30-hour time. I was finally gaining more ground.

"Great," I said, happy to be ahead and know that if I kept moving well, I would get to the finish. I hadn't allowed myself to believe I would finish yet, though. A lot could happen in the next four miles.

We made our way along the single track, in and out of the ripples in the mountain walls, across small creek crossings and erosion control boards. We cruised down the trail and up onto the wider gravel section with a fantastic view of Foresthill Bridge, and soon passed the well-known Training Hill sign.

"We're going to do this," I said to myself. Then I heard the next aid station.

The No Hands Bridge aid station was a party all night. The volunteers decorated the whole aid station with lights and strung them back and forth over the bridge on poles. They adorned the bridge with country flags and played music, making it one of the most fun aid stations to go through.

"Wooo!" I heard someone yell. "Runner coming!" The aid station is on the road below the single-track trail, so the volunteers could see the runners up above as they made their descent to the bridge.

Bob and I made our way down the dusty single track and popped out on the aid station. I had barely drank my Skratch on my way down Rollercoaster so I didn't need a refill at No Hands.

"Keep running," Bob instructed. "I'm grabbing some water."

"1-2-6 in. 1-2-6 out!" I yelled at the volunteers as I made my way over No Hands Bridge. It was quiet after I passed the aid station. It seemed like I was the only one crossing No Hands. Like I was the only one making my way through the canyon. Like I was the only one about to finish Western States. The only thing I could hear was my foot steps pitter pattering across the dirt. And that is the moment I allowed myself to believe I'd actually finish this race. I smiled as I moved along in the warm sunshine.

I ran about halfway across the bridge, then slowed to a walk. I had run almost the whole four miles from Highway 49 aid station to get to this point. I needed to walk.

Then I heard Bob's feet come up alongside me. "Bob, can I walk?" I asked, exhausted.

"You have an hour and 30 minutes to go three miles. You've earned a walk," Bob said with a smile. I smiled back and we marched across No Hands Bridge and up the dusty trail towards the finish.

"I'm going to finish!" I said to Bob excitedly. The reality of the situation was becoming clearer and clearer. I had done the work. I had run the race. I had fought the battle and I was going to finish. Nothing even hurt in that moment. I was elated!

"You're going to finish!" he replied. "But let's make sure we keep moving. We don't want to lose any time."

We walked along at a speedy pace along the river. The water was now on our left with the cliffs to our right. The trail was wide, dry and dusty. There were other runners and pacers making their way towards the finish and we passed a few of them. We crossed the bridge at Calcutta Falls and made our way to the single track that would lead us up to Robie Point. Just before we reached the single track, a familiar face appeared around a corner.

"Ken!" I yelled. Ken had come out to meet us and walk us into the finish. "It's so great to see you again!" I said as I hugged him. It was amazing to have people I knew come find me along the course throughout my race.

"You look amazing! You're making excellent time!" he said to me.

Ken and Bob had run Western States together a few years prior and exchanged some pleasantries as well.

We made a right onto the single track and soon ran into Scott, who had also brought me into Foresthill when I came up Bath Road.

"Scott!" I yelled. "Yay!" He gave me a big hug as he told me I looked great and joined us heading towards Robie Point.

As we made our way up the steepest part of the single track, I started to get really tired and frustrated. Perhaps I was dehydrated, or exhausted. I chugged the rest of my Skratch.

"Gosh I'm thirsty," I said.

"Here, let me give you some water," Scott offered, pulling the top off of his water bottle and pouring half of it into mine.

"Thank you, Scott," I said as I started sipping the cold water. "You're a life saver."

As we came to the top of the steep single track and stepped out onto the fire road, I felt better knowing that we were almost at the finish. Then Bob made us go right at a fork in the trail and we headed up again. I was used to running around Robie Point on the trails, but the actual race course goes up and over on a fire road that continued for what felt like miles straight up.

"Bob!" I yelled, clearly frustrated and over it all. "Are we almost there? Seriously? This is like some cruel joke!"

Bob slowed down next to me and reassuringly said, "Just up this section of the fire road we will be at the Robie Point aid station. Then it's all pavement and people to the finish."

"You better not be lying!" I scolded him. I didn't mean to be so gruff, but my legs were done. My mind was done. I was just DONE. I wanted to be at the track already! The last miles of the race weren't the hardest physically, but they were the most grueling on the mind.

We made our way up a section of the wide, dirt road, and as it curved to the left the aid station came into view.

A volunteer ran down towards me. "What do you need?" he asked. I handed him my bottle and asked for ice water in it and he tore off up the dirt toward the aid station.

Then I saw Kirk, the Robie Point aid station captain, walking down the hill towards me. "Laura! You made it!" he yelled. "Great job!" He walked straight to me and gave me a big hug. We had known each other through our work at Fleet Feet stores and Kirk had run the race a several years before.

"I didn't think I would Kirk!" I said with a sigh. "It's so great to see you!"

He patted me on the back. "But you did!" he said as he continued climbing to the aid station with us.

As we all made our way to the top of Robie Point, the cheers started. Everyone was clapping and yelling for me as I came into the aid station area. That's when I finally saw my crew, pacer and a handful of other friends waiting for me. I smiled when I saw them all and headed right for the aid station. Paul was there, taking photos of me as I came up the last climb. The volunteers, including Karyn, Kathy, Rob and Mary, were so helpful. One of them offered to soak me in ice water, but I told them I didn't want to chafe that close to the finish so I had them cool down my arms instead.

"I'm so happy to be here!" I said as I grabbed some Coke and Sprite from the table.

"We're so happy to see you!" my crew and friends yelled.

I turned around and looked over at them, "You have no idea."

As I peered around at the sea of faces, everything came into a clearer view. I was finishing Western States. And all these people who had been on my journey were here with me for the best part. Joe, Carol and Andy were there. Andy's wife Sarah, and their three kids made it down from Highway 49. Dan and Jennifer were there. They had trained with me on most of my long runs leading up to the race. Of course, Ken and Scott were still there as they had been most of the race. So was Brad, my first pacer. I don't even think he had slept at that point.

"Thank you all!" I called to the aid station. "Thanks Kirk!"

"Great job girl!" he called after me. "Proud of you!"

As we walked out of the aid station with Bob, Brad and I leading the group, everything became crystal clear. I was walking the last mile from Robie Point to Placer High School and I was going to finish this thing. Wow.

"Hey Joe!" I yelled behind me.

"Yeah?" he answered.

"Is your dad at the finish?" I asked.

"Yup," he said. "And your parents."

"They made it?!" I exclaimed.

"Yeah. I introduced them all." My parents hadn't met Joe's dad at that point in our relationship so this, one of the biggest days of my life, was their first meeting. Fitting, I thought.

"Great. Thanks honey," I said, beaming.

We continued my victory march up Robie Drive towards the finish at Placer High School. It was now 10 a.m. With the cutoff being 11 a.m., I knew that no matter what, I could walk to the finish and get my buckle. My mood of the day changed from pure uncertainty to elation! We had done it!

Robie Drive continues straight up the hill until it makes a sharp left and then takes a fork to the right. This area is known as the party zone and is located right at the Western States Mile 99 marker. All of the homeowners decorate the street and come out to cheer on every runner as they come through the last mile of the race. As we came up the road, there were smiles, hugs, high fives and cheers all around us.

"Great job runner!"

"You're almost to the finish!"

"You're amazing!"

That's when I saw her. My coach Mo came running around the corner ahead. She saw me and almost seemed to do a double take before she started screaming.

"Mo! Mo!" I yelled. "I did it Mo! I made it!" The excitement of seeing my coach, coupled with my delirium, was unmatched at this point. I felt the highest high seeing her run towards me to engulf me in a huge, infamous Mo hug.

"You did it girl!" she yelled. "We knew you would!"

"Oh my gosh. I didn't!" I exclaimed as Mo joined my victory parade up Robie Drive.

"Well, it was tough going there for a while. We were worried!" she said with a smile. "But I kept telling Joe to get you moving and tell you to dig deep."

"He did! My crew was so amazing, Mo! And my pacers, Brad and Bob are wonderful. The best," I gushed. I was so happy to have Mo with me on my final mile. She had kept in touch with my crew the whole race, giving instructions and guiding them in helping me finish. She was also our Fleet Feet Sacramento trail coach so she was marking trail and coaching runners the day of the race. I was so glad she had finished in time to join me!

We walked at a nice pace, talking about the race, and joking about wanting a hamburger. At this point, I could actually laugh about what may have been the most stressful 30 hours for my crew. We made the easy right-hand turn from Robie Drive onto Brook Road and continued uphill.

Then I saw someone else running towards us. I couldn't tell who it was until she got closer and started jumping up and down, screaming and pumping her arms. It was Jeanne, one of my running friends from Sacfit!

"You did it girl!" Jeanne screamed as she ran right at me giving me a huge hug. "We're so proud of you!"

"Thanks Jeanne!" I said, "I can't believe it!"

As we marched along more of my friends joined us including Sarah, Candie, Linda, Kathy, Brad, Genna, Dave, Ellisa and Claudia. Everyone was so excited as we made our way up the street.

"Laura, this section has a bit of flat and downhill, let's run some," Mo said, trying to keep my rhythm going so I could run at the finish. I knew I wanted to not only finish strong, but I wanted to run all the way around the Placer High School track to the finish line.

Brook Road made a sweeping left-hand turn and became Channing Way. I was pooped, so I started walking again and the whole group followed my lead. Strangers standing in front of their homes cheered us on and waved as we paraded by.

"This is the best day ever," I said to Mo as tears welled in my eyes.

"You did it girl," Mo said as she put her arm around my shoulder. "We are so proud."

*No crying yet,* I thought to myself, blinking back tears. *Get to the track first.*

We continued straight onto Marvin Way, following the easy curve to the right. I saw a guy and young kid with him ahead of us waving frantically. When I first saw them, I thought it was Andy's friend Af and his son. Then I realized I was wrong, and it was Dusty and his son!

I screamed, "Dusty! I did it!" I took off running down the street and ran right into a huge hug from Dusty. "I did it Dusty! I didn't think I would, but I did it!"

"You did it girl! We are so proud of you!" he said as they continued up the street with us. I was surrounded in people I loved, who loved me. The day couldn't have been more perfect.

"Where's Staci?" I asked, alarmed. Dusty and Staci were due to have their third baby any day and I didn't know if Staci had made the trip up to Auburn or not.

"She's at the stadium, camera ready," he said. "She felt great this morning and said we had to come up and see you finish after watching your valiant effort overnight."

"Yay!" I exclaimed.

We climbed uphill on Marvin Way as it made a left onto Lubeck Road. That's when I saw the white bridge. We all call it the bridge of tears. This is where runners know it's all downhill to the finish. For real. All downhill to the finish. As we began to cross the bridge, my co-worker Cody, who was working the Western States store at the finish line jumped out in front of us.

"Cody!" I yelled as he joined us on the last downhill to the finish at Placer High School.

"Great job girl!" he hollered back.

Our group followed me as I turned left onto Finley Street.

"Laura, it's time to run," Mo instructed.

Knowing full well that I needed to run in the rest of my race, I started at an easy trot with Mo right by my side.

"You've got this girl," she encouraged. "You are there already. You've done all the work and this is your moment."

I couldn't believe we were making the final push to the finish of one of the most prestigious races in the world. The Western States Endurance Run.

"Keep good form," Mo said. "Everyone will be taking pictures of you. It's time to focus on using less energy and smiling. You got this." I laughed at her knowing she was being completely serious. After almost 30 hours of running, your form is shot.

"I want you all to run around the track with me!" I yelled back at my group of friends. "I couldn't have done this without you! It's our victory lap!"

"You got it!" they all cheered.

We cruised down Finley Street as it wound through the homes of Auburn. Hundreds of runners had made this same trek to the bottom of Finley where the Placer High School track awaited them. As we approached the bottom, there was a huge group of spectators right outside of the stadium. They all began screaming as we came down the road. I glanced at my watch. We were running a 10:30 pace at mile 100 of Western States.

*This is insane!* I thought.

"There it is, Laura," Mo yelled at me over the screaming, as she pointed at the track. "You lead the way in!"

I stepped in front of her and made a bee-line for the Placer High School track gate. I cruised through, made the right-hand turn down the ramp and the left-hand turn onto the track.

*We are here!* I thought. *300 yards to glory!*

The track was well worn from years and years of track meets and football games at PHS. I like to think it was from years and years of Western States finishers and their friends and family running on it. We could hear the announcer on the other side of the track introducing runners coming down the finishing chute. Mo was on my left as we cruised along.

When we entered the track more of my running friends joined us, including Ken, Kathy and Tim. I had a smile glued to my face as we made our way down the first straight away of the 300-yard loop to the finish. I couldn't believe we were running on the track! *I made it!* I thought. Mo ran alongside me and continued reminding me to run strong as I finished my biggest race ever. We began to take the left-hand curve at the top of the track and I saw my friend Annie right ahead of me with her phone out filming us. She was screaming loudly, "Yeah girl!"

Just then my pacer Brad moved up on my right. "You are killing it girl! The finish is right there!" he said with a smile. He was running in his sandals as we neared the finish. What a trooper!

I couldn't stop smiling as we reached the end of the curve and neared the beginning of the finisher's chute.

"Take it girl! Go!" Mo yelled at me, clapping and outstretching her hand to point down the chute.

I took off running as my crew, pacers and friends peeled off to the right. I ran solo down the last 50 yards of the course. I couldn't wipe the gigantic smile off my face. I high-fived spectators on my left as I made my way down the final stretch. Tropical John, the announcer, read my name and some of my accolades as I neared the finish line.

About 10 yards from the finish I threw my hands up in the air and glanced up at the clock and Western States banner. I had done it. All of the hard work. All of the uncertainty of the race. All of the hard parts, and the moments that came naturally. I had done it. Every single step was mine. The last few strides through the finish line were in slow motion and felt like magic. I did it.

Once I was clear of the finish and the chip mats, I dropped my hands and bent to put them on my knees.

"Congratulations!" a man said as he put a medal around my neck and gave me a hug.

"Thank you so much!" I responded, elated that I had finished. I had really done it!

"Holy heck!" I said as I bent over again to catch my breath. I took a few photos holding up my medal and that's when the reality really set in.

*Did I just finish Western States?* I thought. *For reals?*

I had. I had pushed through the mountains and canyons. I had beat the altitude and pushed up steep climbs in temperatures reaching 100 degrees. I had crossed rivers and streams, battled exhausting night-time hours and long, hot and humid daylight. I had spent a year and a half training for this exact race. I had spent hours and hours of my life running back and forth through the mountains of California to eventually reach this finish line.

I had finished the Western States Endurance Run in 29:17:36.

I am a Western States finisher. And no one can ever take that away from me.

♦ ♦ ♦

As I moved through the finishing area, a volunteer handed me a bottle of water. Just past her I saw my friend Andrea standing on the other side of the fence. I walked right to her as she engulfed me in a huge hug. We both burst into tears. We had run Javelina Jundred together the year before and this was a culmination of many miles run together over the years. Candie and Kathleen were both there too.

After that I went over and hugged Annie, then Dusty and gave his son a high five. Mo came up and found me along with both my pacers, Brad and Bob. Then I finally made my way across to Joe on the other side of the chute. Brad, Ellisa, Amanda and Diane also smothered me in hugs and appreciation.

My parents and friends Andi, John and Sandy were all waiting inside the fence near the medical research study tent. I had agreed to participate in the medical research study that year, so we all exchanged hugs as I was whisked away for a massage, blood draw, blood pressure reading and weigh in. While in the tent, Andy briefed my parents, Andi, John and Sandy, and a few of my other friends with all the tales of my adventure through the mountains.

After my obligations with the medical study, I got to say hello to Staci, Angie, Scott and Joe's dad, Ron. Joe brought me some breakfast of pancakes, bacon and eggs as I rested in the shade with my family. The medal ceremony took place a few hours after the 11 a.m. cutoff for the race. Joe led me over to the bathrooms so I could get cleaned up and change into clean clothes and flip-flops.

Joe waited for me outside of the bathroom. After giving myself a "baby wipe bath" and changing into clean clothes, I gingerly walked out, looking at him with a weak smile.

"Gosh I'm sore," I said to him.

"That's to be expected. Do you need my help?"

"No, let's just take it slow," I responded. I luckily didn't have any blisters. I had a bit of chafing on my legs and my muscles felt like they had been pulverized, but come hell or high water I was going to walk to that awards ceremony to get my buckle.

I slowly made my way to the tent across the lawn. I took a seat in one of the camp chairs my crew had set up as more of my friends stopped by to congratulate me. Kelly showed up then with flowers and a bag of Birthday Cake Oreos, which had become a post-big-race tradition for the two of us. She gave me a hug and sat down on my lap.

"I'm so proud of you!" she said with tears in her eyes.

"Thanks Kel. I can't believe I did it!" I responded.

"I knew you would. We tried to wait for you at Dusty Corners."

"I know, Joe told me. It's totally OK," I said. I could tell she was bummed.

"And I fell asleep and missed your finish. I'm sorry."

"It's really OK. I know someone got it on film," I laughed.

The awards ceremony started by recognizing the male and female winners, the top 10 in both gender and the oldest male and female finishers. After that, all finishers were named in order of their finishing time. I was in the very last group since I finished in the final hour of the race. When they called for the 29-hour group to assemble next to the tent, I slowly made my way to the left side waiting for my name and time to be called.

"In a time of 29:17, Laura Langerwerf," the announcer said.

I smiled so big and made my way gingerly across the tent, shaking the hands of Tim Twietmeyer (25-time Western States finisher, and five-time winner), along with several of the board members. There I collected my buckle from one of them. This year the organizers had engraved our names on the back of our buckles in real time. As I walked out of the award area, I saw my crew and a few friends waiting on the other side to congratulate me. I held my buckle up for a photo and hugged everyone.

It felt like magic to hold that buckle in my hands. It signified so many hard hours spent on the trail. So much grit. So much heart. And a will to never, ever give up.

I did exactly what I came to Western States to accomplish.

I finished.

And I earned every single bit of it.

# EIGHTEEN
## Get to the Sunshine

It never occurred to me until after the fact, that running 100 miles is like navigating life. There are so many things you learn over time that change you and shape you into the person you are meant to be. Running 100 miles is like that. You don't realize how many things you will go through that will make or break you. Lessons you learn that will push you to your limits. Things you will experience that will make you question everything you thought you knew.

Robin Arzon, a One Peloton instructor, said it best when she wrote, "Running parallels life in the most basic ways. How much can you give? How much heart do you have?" In running, change happens when we are uncomfortable. Change happens when we push our limits. Change doesn't happen when we keep doing the same thing over and over again. The same is true in life. We only get better at things when we push ourselves to learn more, try harder and step out of our comfort zone.

How much can you give? Probably more than you think you can. You just have to ask it of your body and mind and trust you will be able to give a little more each time. How much heart do you have? I bet you have a lot more than you think you do. You have much more inside your brain and body than you realize. It's a matter of tapping into your physical and mental potential to reach your best self.

So, what did I learn about life in running 100 miles?

## 1. When things happen in life that you can't change, you have to roll with the punches.

In running 100 miles, things happen that force you to abandon your original plan and fight through to the end. When I underestimated the difficulty of Western States and the toll altitude running would take on my body, I couldn't just throw in the towel. I had worked too hard to get to the start line and I wasn't about to give that up. I had to reevaluate and move forward one step at a time towards my goal. I had to move to plan B and eventually plan C in real time as I evaluated my status with every step.

In life, rolling with the punches is something we have to do. We have to take the bad times and then find a new road around them. When my friend Cathy had her accident, she chose to fight and move forward. She has continued to show that perseverance and drive in her life daily. Cathy has reached new goals and achieved many things in her recovery that we can't even dream of. When she was knocked down, she got up and made the best of what she had been given. She is an example of what hard work and dedication can do for you, no matter what situation you are in. Cathy is not a victim of her circumstances. She embraces them and moves forward with a bright future. Cathy inspired me to start running and with those first miles set me on a path that would lead me to running this race. I know that her accident was part of my story, and while none of us wanted it to happen, I know that good can come from bad if you choose to see the bright side.

## 2. When you feel like you've been beaten down, lower than you ever could be, look around you. There are people just waiting to help pick you up.

When I left Robinson Flat during Western States, I was toast. My body hurt, my brain ached, and I was dehydrated. The altitude had knocked me down terribly. Then I began climbing out of the aid station and saw John Trent, then Western States President. He smiled at me and told me I could make it. I knew who he was and knew that he wouldn't have put that confidence in me if he thought I really wasn't going to make it to Miller's Defeat. When I was falling apart, a stranger encouraged me to not give up and pushed me to work harder. My crew offered the same guidance. All day and night they kept pumping me up, even when they might have thought that there wasn't a chance I would succeed. They pushed me to reach further than I thought I could.

In my race, I chose to take what John and my crew told me and believe I could finish the race. I chose to not let being knocked down define me. Just like in life. When my engagement ended, so many supportive people surrounded me. I was crushed more than I ever had been in my life. But those people picked me up. They didn't let me sit and wallow in self-pity. They made sure I was OK and got me moving on the path to emotional recovery. We can't allow the things that knock us down define who we are. Just because we find ourselves in situations that tear us down, it doesn't mean we have to stay there. It doesn't mean we have to be a victim. We can strive to be better, strive to rise above and strive to work even harder to reach our goals.

## 3. Some things in life are meant to change in order to put you on a better path.

When I planned to run Western States, I naively thought I would be able to complete the race in 27 or 28 hours. After all, I had finished my first 100 in 28 hours so I figured that since I had trained so hard on the actual course, I would be able to do even better at Western States. However, when I began moving at that altitude, I quickly realized that I would not be able to reach that goal. And that I would have to abandon my plans and just try to survive in the race.

When I was laid off from my job, I had to do the same thing. I thought I would work at the agency for a long time. I believed that I would stay in advertising for the rest of my life. Losing my job taught me that the best laid plans aren't always the plans you should follow. When life's path reaches a fork in the road, know that you can take the road less traveled and make something new for yourself. When it seems like you are alone and starting from nothing, know that if you believe in yourself, you can do anything. It's a choice you have to make. Choose to leave everything you have on the table and do something you haven't before. Life is not supposed to be easy, but it is supposed to teach us things in the easy and hard times. We just have to absorb the moments and choose to work hard and learn from them.

4. God has a plan for all of us. We just have to follow His signs to get to where He wants us to be.

During Western States, I had to have faith in myself and know that God had a plan for me that day. He knew I would make it to the end and would learn so much in the process. He knew it would be hard and He would push me, but God also knew it wouldn't be an easy road to get there. When I reached No Hands Bridge at mile 97 and could walk the last 3 miles to the finish, a calm came over me. I knew there were three miles left, but I knew we could get there. I knew I would finish, and I knew the crazy race I had run was all part of His plan. I knew there were so many lessons learned, but the biggest one was to have faith in myself.

When I met Joe, it was difficult to go through a breakup and eventually a make up. I had to trust that God had a plan and this was all part of it. He has a grand plan for all of us. We have to have faith that we will reach whatever He has planned, whether we like the path or not. There have been many ups and downs in my life. Back and forth, two steps forward, one step back. But all of those moments have led me to the life I now live. It took me a very long time to understand that I needed to go through all the trials and tribulation to appreciate the life I am blessed with today.

5. Hard work and dedication are simply a part of life.

In 100 miles you have to keep pushing forward even when you don't want to, because there's no one else that can run the race but you. Yes, you have a crew. Yes, you have pacers. Yes, you have friends and family cheering you on. But when you run 100 miles, no one else can take all of those steps but you. It sounds heavy, and it should. You must have a no-quit attitude. And you must rely on those around you to support you, while you take every single step yourself.

Life is not easy. My eighth grade teacher, Mr. Brandol, used to always say, "If life were easy, I'd be seven-feet tall and in the NBA." Life isn't easy, but it teaches us lessons along the way. And the greatest is that we have to do the work. Growing up on a farm taught me that no one else can live our life but us. No one can work for what we want, except us. No one can make things happen for us, we have to take the steps to do it. We have to work hard every day for everything we earn. And while the hard work is unrelenting, in the end, the reward pays off.

## 6. Taking care of your body also takes care of your mind. When you get healthy, amazing things happen.

At Western States, I was in the best shape of my life. I was strong, fit, healthy and mentally focused. I was confident and secure in my abilities. Before I started, I was sure I could run this race and finish. I went in with that mentality because I was physically and mentally ready for the task. And when things went awry, I was strong and resilient. And I relied on my body and mind to get me through the tough parts. Being healthy takes care of your mind and body in more ways than you can even imagine. And it sets you up for success before you even start working towards something. I've found that being physically and mentally healthy has made so many aspects of my life successful. And that makes me a stronger person all around. I know I can do anything I put my mind to.

Being healthy changes your world. When you reset your body and your mind you can achieve anything. We are what we eat, drink and do, so being the healthiest we can not only helps us achieve our goals and dreams, it also makes us the best version of ourselves to do those things. When I started working out, managed my weight, learned to be healthy and began my running career, it changed my entire perspective on what I could and couldn't do. If I can do this, I can do more. If I can do that, I can do more. Getting healthy allowed me to work harder, feel better, sleep sounder and made my goals seem much more possible than they ever had before.

## 7. When it may not seem like the path you want to take, you just have to believe and take it anyway.

Before I ran Western States, I told my coach, "I will never run 100 miles. That is insane." Now I've done it twice. Who would have thought I would become an ultra-marathon runner? Who would have even thought I would become a marathon runner before I moved to Sacramento? I sure didn't. But the path I didn't want to take, inevitably put me somewhere I needed to be, to end up in this life.

When forks are put in the road of life, you have to choose a path and know you will learn something and find the place you should be on in the process. You can't fight opportunities in life because you may find something you never thought you would enjoy. Sure, you can hate it when you get there, but staying open to the idea is so important because what you get out of it may be far more than you ever thought it would be.

8. "The definition of insanity is doing the same thing over and over, and expecting a different result." – Albert Einstein

While running Western States I couldn't just keep doing everything I had done over and over again. I couldn't just walk the hills whenever I wanted to. I couldn't stop and rest when I wanted to. Every minute counted so I had to stop doing the same thing over and over again and push myself to be better and work harder. When I was on the course, Brad and Bob made me do things I didn't want to do. They made me step outside of my comfort zone and push harder than I thought I could. Their faith in me allowed me to believe I could do all the things my brain was telling me I couldn't.

Let's be real. I'm a slow runner. I'm a back of the packer. I always say, "I am the sweeper, I pick up the dead bodies." When I first heard that from one of the folks in the movie "Spirit of the Marathon," I laughed because it's so true. I'm a slow runner, and I'm OK with that most of the time. In my training I had to change some things to be stronger. I had to run the hill repeats I didn't want to run. I had to get comfortable with being uncomfortable. It was hard, but it was worth it. And in life I've learned that doing the things you don't want to is part of your journey. It will either teach you a lesson, be a positive experience or teach you something you don't want to repeat later. But you can't just avoid those things because you don't like them.

*Get to the Sunshine* is not just about reaching the sunshine in a 100 miler. It's also about reaching the sunshine on the other side of challenges in our lives. Finding the purpose in those difficult parts of our life and understanding how they will affect us moving forward.

In any situation there could be darkness, but just as there are rainbows after the storm, there is always sunshine after night. Just get to the sunshine and you will be on the other side.

Western States is 29 hours and 17 minutes that changed my life for the better. It showed me what I was made of. It taught me that hard work will yield great results if you have the heart to push yourself further than you ever have before. It showed me that the love of a community will always amaze you, even more than you already think it does.

Western States will always have my heart. It's a monumental race in my running career and an experience I will never forget. Every time I venture to the Western States trail for a training run or hike, I'm taken back to that day and all the things it revealed for me in my life.

It's not the destination, but the journey. And that, my friends, was a well-fought journey.

# RACE PHOTOS

Western States Endurance Run
Class of 2015 photo
This was used on the live
stream for race tracking

At the start line of the
2015 Western States
Endurance Run

Climbing the Escarpment in the first miles of the race

Climbing over the Escarpment – approximately mile 3.5

Running down the back side of the Escarpment

Running down to Duncan Creek – approximately mile 27

Coming into
Robinson Flat
Aid Station –
approximately
mile 30

Dusty Corners Aid Station with Joe – approximately mile 38

Just past Devil's Thumb Aid Station, near The Pump, I ran into my first running coach who gave me some words of encouragement – approximately mile 48

Making my way through the aid station in Michigan Bluff – approximately mile 55

Receiving the royal pit crew treatment from Carol in Foresthill – approximately mile 62

At the Ford's Bar Aid Station with my pacer Brad – approximately mile 73

Leaving Auburn Lake Trails Aid Station with my pacer Bob – approximately mile 85

Climbing up Robie Point with friends – approximately mile 98

Hiking out of the Robie Point Aid Station – approximately mile 99

Walking the last mile with friends, training partners, pacers, crew and my coach

Running into Placer High School

Coming to the finish chute

Finish line of the 2015 WSER – official finish time 29:17:36

Buckle Ceremony with
Tim Twietmeyer

Official Western States
Endurance Run finisher

Laura and Kelly after the Buckle Ceremony

Laura with Cathy (left) and Kira at her wedding in 2016

# ACKNOWLEDGEMENTS

My dear friend, Carol Falter, lost her battle with cancer prior to publication of this book. She was such a light in my life and a true friend. Carol had the heart of a teacher and was the most giving soul I've ever known. She stood by me through tough times and joined me in celebrating my accomplishments. Carol blessed all who knew her with her presence, knowledge and unforgettable laugh. I would not have gotten through the Western States race without her by my side. I will love and miss you always, Carol.

Maureen Bartley, known to us as Mo, is the most amazing coach. She got me to that finish line with her kind words, no-nonsense personality and coaching skill that took what I had to work with and turned it into a 100-mile runner. Mo made me run hills when I didn't want to and gave me grace when I needed to take a day off. She is a wonderful member of the ultra running community and we should all consider ourselves lucky to know her. Thank you for your guidance and heart, Mo.

Brad De Luchi and Bob Halpenny, my amazing pacers. The miles we spent together were tough, but worth every single step. Thank you for listening to me whine and still pushing me to move. Thank you for knowing when to let off the gas and when to step on it. Thank you for guiding me to the finish I had always dreamed of. You are both amazing people and I cherish your friendship and guidance so much more than I can ever put into words.

Andy Solari, my crew would have been missing a huge piece without you. Your continued support and friendship in running brings so much joy to my life. You have been a great friend since our days editing advertising proposals together. And yes, I will always use my stern voice with you when making changes. Thank you for supporting me and continuing to push me to run when I don't want to. It makes me so happy to see you loving this sport as much, if not more, than I do.

When I started working at Fleet Feet Sacramento in 2013, I had no idea it would take me to the places I've been. Before then it had just been the store I visited when I needed a new pair of shoes or some running gear. But this place became so much more than that for me. Thank you to Dusty for offering me an interview, and to Pat for offering me a job. Thank you for trusting me to work for your amazing company for three years and providing me with the opportunity to run Western States. Your belief in me and my abilities truly helped me to make it through each of the lows in this race. I can't thank Dusty and Staci Robinson and Pat and Jan Sweeney enough for everything they've given me in my years as a runner. I'm proud to be a lifelong member of The Originals.

I started my running career with Sacfit. It was where I met my best friend Kelly, and where I learned much of what I know about running. Sacfit has been there when my world has fallen apart and seen me through some of my best experiences. Sacfit brought me to this amazing sport of running. My first Sacfit head coach, Ken, has been there for late-night training runs, as well as long Saturdays and Sundays in the canyons of California. Through our conversations, Ken reminds me I have what it takes to be a great ultra runner, and he had the guts to be the first person to tell me I could run 100 miles. Ken, thank you for your continued guidance, support and friendship. And for making Sacfit a home for so many of us.

Kelly Valentine. What can I say? It's been a heck of a ride so far! I consider myself one of the luckiest people on this earth to have you as a friend. You give and give and give and don't expect anything in return. You support those around you and offer guidance to people who need help, all with a smile and a hug along the way. Thank you for being such a huge part of both my running and life journey. Your support, kindness and friendship mean the world to me and I look forward to so many more years of laughs, meals and miles getting dirty on the trails. I love you friend.

My best friend since college, Alexis Nascimento, took on the task of editing this book for me. She had no idea what she was getting into, and knew literally nothing about trail running or ultras, for that matter. But she took it on anyway and helped me put together a story I am so, so proud of. Thank you for being honest and loving, while still telling me when I needed to push harder. Thank you for knowing I could handle criticism and for reminding me that I am a good writer. All those years in journalism classes with you apparently paid off. I love you BFF.

Cathy Liu is the reason I started running. While her accident wasn't something anyone saw coming, she has made the outcome into something positive. Thank you, Cathy, for continuing to support me in my adventures and for sharing your story with all of us. You are an inspiration to so many and we cherish all the memories we've made with you over the years. I will continue to run miles for you and look forward to running with you someday.

Mom, Dad and my family. Thank you for teaching me what hard work looks like. Thank you for making me get up early on the weekends to help around the house. Thank you for not letting things slide when I got an attitude with you. Thank you for instilling perseverance in me and my brother and making us the hard workers we are today. Thank you for helping me raise animals and learn the ropes of farming. Thank you for showing me how family supports each other and how to be a good, giving friend. Thank you for loving me when my life was broken and helping me pick up the pieces. And thank you for making the trip to see me cross that finish line. Knowing you got to see me achieve this goal brings me so much happiness in my life as a runner. I love you guys.

Joe, Jacob and Ellie. You are all blessings I never expected to have. Jacob, when I first wrote this book, you were too small to know the impact you've had on my life. Let me tell you, the impact is a big one. You made me a mama. You bless our days with your energy and zest for life. Ellie, you are a blessing we didn't know we would receive. But we are so thankful for your excitement and true joy for all things in life. May you know how loved you are, how strong you are, and that you can do anything you put your mind to in this life. If you two just believe and work hard, you can do anything. We love you and are proud of you both.

Joe, you are the best thing that has ever happened to me. My life has taken on a new level of amazing since the day I met you. Thank you for supporting me. Thank you for making me feel loved. Thank you for always telling me I can dream big, even when I have to remind you I'm dreaming. Thank you for just wanting us to be happy in our life. I love our life and the adventure we are on together. I can't wait to see where it takes us next. I love you most.

To everyone else mentioned in this book, thank you for being a part of my life and my journey. You've made me the person I am today and I am grateful for all the good, bad and ugly we've been through. We all have a path and a story we follow and I consider myself very lucky to have had all of you along for the ride.

A special thank you to the people who helped me make this book.

Author Headshot - Jill Anderson Photography

Cover Photo - Kelly Valentine

Cover and Map Design - Anna Martin Design

Editing – Alexis Nascimento

# ABOUT THE AUTHOR

Laura Chancellor is a stay-at-home mom in El Dorado Hills, California. She married her husband Joe in 2016 and they have two kids named Jacob and Ellie. She grew up on a dairy farm in Durham, California, attended Chico State University and majored in Journalism with the option in Public Relations. She lived and worked in the Sacramento advertising/public relations/marketing industry for 12 years before relocating to where they live now.

Laura has been running endurance events including marathons since 2008 and regularly running ultramarathon distance events since 2013. She has completed more than 10 marathons, a combined fifteen 50Ks and 50 milers, a 100k finish and three 100-mile races. She works part-time as a running coach. She continues to be a part of the ultramarathon community and hopes to expand her coaching business in the future. Laura has her sights set on toeing the line at Western States again someday.

Connect with Laura on the following platforms:
Instagram: @LauraCRuns
Facebook: @lauralchancellor
YouTube: Laura Chancellor

# NOTES

This list includes films, products, quotes, etc. mentioned within this book.

Unbreakable. 2011 documentary film. Directed by JB Benna. Distributed and produced by Journeyfilm. 2011. Released November 22, 2012.

Western States Endurance Run website: WSER.org

Skratch Labs Hydration Drink Mix
Made by Skratch Labs. The casual reference I use is "Skratch", thus the reason I call it Skratch throughout the book. Learn more about their products at skratchlabs.com

Western Time | a Western States 100 Film. 2014 documentary film. Directed and produced by Billy Yang. Distributed by Billy Yang Films on YouTube. Released November 11, 2014.

Albert Einstein – "The definition of insanity is doing the same thing over and over, and expecting a different result."

Robin Arzon. One Peloton Vice President and Instructor. Instagram @robinnyc. April 15, 2019.
 https://www.instagram.com/p/BwS1Ly_FT95/

Spirit of the Marathon. 2007 documentary film directed by Jon Dunham. Produced by Mark Jonathan Harris, Gwendolen Twist, Jon

Dunham. Distributed by Image Entertainment. Released October 5, 2007.